9th Cavalry

10th Cavalry

11th Armored Cavalry

12th Cavalry

13th Cavalry

14th Armored Cavalry

15th Cavalry

16th Armor

17th Cavalry

U.S. Armor-Cavalry (1917-1967)

A Short History

by Duncan Crow
Editor AFV/Weapons series

Profile Publications Limited
Windsor, Berkshire, England

Other Profile Books

AFV/Weapons Series

1   Modern US Armored Support Vehicles

2   British and Commonwealth Armoured Formations (1919–46)

3   79th Armoured Division: Hobo's Funnies

4   In Trust for the Nation: HMS *Belfast* 1939–1971

Other Famous Profile Bound Volume Series

AFVs of the World:

Volume 1 World War I 1914–1919

Volume 2 British AFVs 1919–1940

Volume 3 British and Commonwealth AFVs 1940–1946

Volume 4 American AFVs of World War II

Aircraft in Profile: Volumes 1-11

Locomotives in Profile: Volumes 1-2

Warships in Profile: Volumes 1-2

1SBN 0 85383 084 3

First published in 1973, by
PROFILE PUBLICATIONS LIMITED
Windsor, Berkshire, England

Printed in England by Edwin Snell printers, Yeovil, Somerset

Contents

Acknowledgements

The Author and Publisher wish to acknowledge the kind assistance given by the United States Army, the United States Marine Corps, and especially by Colonel Robert J. Icks, Army of the United States (Retd.) without whose help this book could not have been produced. They would also like to thank the Office, Chief of Military History, Department of the Army, for permission to reproduce the U.S. Armor-Cavalry regimental coats of arms and historic badges, and to thank those who made photographs available through Colonel Icks.

About the Author

DUNCAN CROW is a military and social historian. Since January 1969 he has been the Editor of Profile's AFV/Weapons series and also acts as General Military Editor for the Publisher. Duncan Crow was born in Aberdeen (Scotland), educated in Edinburgh, Grenoble, London, and the Army. He served throughout the 1939–45 war, joining the Royal Armoured Corps in September 1939. He served with the Mine Design Department, HMS *Vernon;* then with the Royal Tank Regiment; was commissioned in the 5th Royal Inniskilling Dragoon Guards. He was in charge of the Wireless Wing at the 56th Training Regt., RAC, and then Assistant Chief Instructor of the Regiment. He served with the famous Phantom Intelligence (GHQ Liaison Regt.) in the North-West Europe campaign from Normandy to Hamburg, attached to First Canadian Army and Third U.S. Army. Was present at the liberation of Buchenwald and Ohrdruf Camps, April 1945. On staff of Khaki University of Canada in England, 1945–1946.

Subsequently Duncan Crow became a professional writer and researcher, gaining wide experience and a high reputation.
From 1958 to 1970 he worked with Granada Television as writer, researcher, producer, executive. One of the original World in Action producers, 1963.

Has written and had published twelve books to date, covering a wide range of subjects – both fiction and non-fiction.

French Renault F.T. tank of the 1st (later 304th) U.S. Tank Brigade during an attack on October 7, 1918 in the Meuse-Argonne offensive.
(U.S. Signal Corps Photo No. 111–SC–27424 in the National Archives)

U.S. Armored Organization

by Duncan Crow

I
(TO 1918)

BY the time the United States of America became a World War I belligerent in April 1917, tanks had already made their appearance on the battlefield. The British had used them first on the Somme on September 15, 1916, and now had 27 operational tank companies organized in nine battalions. The French had ten tank companies and used eight of them in their first tank action on April 16, 1917.

Interest in armored fighting vehicles already existed on a minor scale in the United States before 1917—though hardly at all in military circles. As in several other countries the first tentative AFVs had been armored cars.

The first American armored car was only partially armored. Designed by Colonel R. P. Davidson of the

Illinois National Guard in 1898 it was a Colt automatic gun with a steel shield, mounted on a three-wheeled Duryea passenger runabout. This was followed by two steam-driven cars built by cadets at the Northwestern Military and Naval Academy of which Davidson was commandant. The performance of these two cars on a road run from Chicago to Washington sufficiently impressed Lieutenant-General Nelson A. Miles on the eve of his retirement as Commanding General of the Army in 1903 for him to recommend to the Secretary of War that five of the fifteen cavalry regiments be converted to an automobile corps. Nothing, however, came of this first suggestion for cavalry mechanization, and indeed it was not until 1916 that motorization arrived initially in the United States Army.

Colonel Davidson continued his development of armored cars and in 1915 produced the first true armored car in the United States. The following year the first American armored units appeared. Two Regular Army units were formed for duty on the Mexican border. One was equipped with armored Jeffery Quad trucks known as Armored Cars No. 1, the other with armored White trucks known as Armored Cars No. 2; both units also had motor-cycle machine-guns.

The New York National Guard also formed an armored unit, the 1st Armored Motor Battery, which served on the Mexican border equipped with three armored cars, staff cars, trucks and motor-cycle machine-guns; and the Michigan National Guard, another of the great number of National Guard units that were called into Federal service for patrol duty along the Mexican border, took an improvized Reo armored car with them.

Although the Punitive Expedition into Mexico that resulted from Pancho Villa's raid was principally a horsed cavalry action, "the last such in American history," as the official history of Armor-Cavalry relates*, this force, under Major-General John J. Pershing, was an important harbinger, for it introduced motor trucks as part of the supply system. Although these trucks caused concern among their protagonists, and quiet jubilation among their opponents, because of frequent mechanical breakdown—reactions that were standard in all armies throughout the world whenever and wherever the horse was threatened by the internal combustion engine—their appearance on the military scene began the inexorable domination of the machine as a means of military transport and as a fighting vehicle in the U.S. Army.

By this time the inventors were busy in the United States as elsewhere in developing the tracklaying type of

---

* p. 34 Armor-Cavalry Part I: Regular Army and Army Reserve, by Mary Lee Stubbs and Stanley Russell Connor. Office Chief of Military History, 1969. (Army Lineage Series.)

AFV—the tank. There was an idea once current—and perhaps still is in some places—that inventions come from what has been called "the hermit genius, spinning inventions out of his intellectual and psychic innards." There is little truth in this. Inventions, like scientific research, are in fact a social phenomenon. The social climate and social institutions have to be sympathetic for them to flourish; and indeed so much are research and invention a social phenomenon that there are fashions in them just as there are fashions in clothes. Trench warfare, on the scale that solidified the Western Front from September 1914, created a fashion for armed and armored tracklayers—vehicles that, for security reasons in the first place, were given the non-commital cover name of "tanks".

Early tank operations on the Western Front were far from wholly successful. One result of this was that the American Military Mission in Paris, which had been directed to examine the use of tanks by the British and the French, drew more attention to the tanks' defects than to the new opportunities they offered for breaking the stalemate on the Western Front and declared them a failure. The Military Mission's report, dated May 21, 1917, reflected an attitude very similar to that of the German High Command. Both regarded the failure of the tank to make a decisive impact as something that was attributable to an inherent fault in the weapon itself, instead of recognizing—as its supporters did—that the failure was the result of the weapon's misuse.

But the lukewarm report of the Military Mission had no ultimate effect on policy. Soon after General Pershing's arrival in France on June 13, 1917, as Commander-in-Chief, American Expeditionary Forces (AEF), the tank and its possibilities were studied in

In 1916 the New York National Guard 1st Armored Motor Battery used this Locomobile Armored Car, one of three similar cars of different makes.
(Courtesy C. W. Sutton)

The C. L. Best tractor was the basis of this simulated tank, one of several American experiments in the tracklaying type of AFV, seen here with elements of the California National Guard in San Francisco in 1917. (Outlook Magazine)

great detail by several committees reporting to a board at AEF GHQ. The principal conclusions were that the tank was a factor which was "destined to become an important element in this war:" that a heavy and a light model should be used; and that there should be a separate tank service.

Based on these recommendations the Project for the Overseas Tank Corps was drafted. The Corps was to consist of five heavy tank battalions equipped with tanks of the British heavy type, and twenty light tank battalions equipped with tanks of the French light Renault F.T. type (then in course of production). Pershing approved the Project on September 23, 1917.

By this time several experimental tanks had been built by American companies, and others had been proposed by American inventors. In the event none of these became the equipment for the new American tank force. Instead, for the heavy tank, the British Mark VI was proposed and 600 were provisionally ordered; and for the light tank a modified Renault was to be produced in the United States.

The Mark VI, designed by Major W. G. Wilson and with a Ricardo engine, existed only as a wooden model. Although it had longer ground contact than previous Marks this increased length was not considered sufficient, nor the engine powerful enough, for Western Front conditions by the two U.S. Ordnance Department officers, Majors Alden and Drain, who were appointed by Pershing in October to study the design and construction of British tanks in detail. In December the provisional order for the Mark VIs was cancelled—indeed no Mark VI was ever built—and in its place a

An early American-built tank was this Holt Gas-Electric prototype of 1917. The three-quarter left rear view does not show the 75-mm mountain gun which was mounted in the nose. Each side sponson mounted a Browning machine-gun, not installed in this photograph.

(U.S. Ordnance Department)

The Skeleton Tank of 1917 built by the Pioneer Tractor Company was an attempt to achieve trench-crossing ability combined with lightness and cheapness. It never went into production.

(Courtesy Col. G. B. Jarrett)

British Mark V tanks of the 301st Battalion, 2nd (later 305th) U.S. Tank Brigade, flying the Stars and Stripes on their way forward to the Battle of the Selle in October 1918. (U.S. Signal Corps)

Two U.S. Signal Corps cameramen riding on the sponson of a British Mark IV supply tank of the 2nd (later 305th) U.S. Tank Brigade during the Storming of the Hindenburg Line at the end of September 1918 when the brigade first saw combat. (U.S. National Archives)

Fifteen thousand of these little Ford Two-Man tanks, designed by the U.S. Ordnance Department and weighing three tons, were ordered. Only 15 were finished before the order was cancelled after the Armistice in November 1918. (Col. R. J. Icks)

tank treaty was signed in January 1918 under which another new model, the Mark VIII, with longer ground contact and twice the engine power of the Mark VI, would be built jointly in large numbers by the United States, Britain, and France. The United States would build the engines, transmissions, and track parts; Britain was to provide armor, track plates, and armament; while France was to erect the assembly plant. This plan did not work out. The German March offensive, the strain on British industry, and the inability of American industry to produce the Liberty engines in sufficient quantity were among the factors that delayed production to such a degree that no Mark VIIIs were ready in time to take part in the war.

Nor were there faster results in the light tank program. By the time of the Armistice on November 11, 1918, no American-built tanks had reached the U.S. Tank Corps in France. The first ten Six-Ton M1917 tanks, as the American version of the Renault FT was called, arrived at the end of the month. Had the war continued, however, there would have been a different story to tell. The long lead time inherent in tank production was over and the factories were about to start delivering their full output.

American-built Mark VIII tanks after they had been withdrawn from service in the 1930s. (U.S. Army)

In the event, of course, this full output was aborted. Orders were cancelled, development ceased. Even so, by mid-1919 the Tank Corps had 863 American-built tanks and, after 300 more had been delivered on outstanding contracts, 1,163. Though too late for World War I these had still a vital part to play, for they were the mainstay of American armored training in the inter-war years: between 1920 and 1935 only 35 new tanks were built. Furthermore many of them were to become the mechanical foundation of another great armored force. In 1940 they were sold to Canada at a nominal price as training vehicles for the budding Canadian Armoured Corps.

THE UNITED STATES TANK CORPS

At the same time as the equipment for the new arm of the U.S. Army was being ordered, General Pershing developed the plans for a tank corps in the AEF. Its size was based on a projected expeditionary force of 20 combat divisions. There were to be a General Headquarters and 25 tank battalions—five of them heavy, the remainder light. The planned number of heavy battalions was subsequently increased to 10. In addition there were to be 10 brigades, three tank centers, and two army tank HQ. All the units were to be under command of GHQ, Tank Corps, and would then be allotted to armies or lower formations for specific operations, on the completion of which they would revert to GHQ control. An army tank HQ consisted of an HQ and a heavy mobile ordnance repair shop and was intended to work at an army HQ level. The brigades were operational commands. The function of the tank center was to train personnel and provide reinforcements.

On December 22, 1917, Colonel Samuel D. Rockenbach, a Quartermaster officer with over 20 years' cavalry service, was appointed Chief of the Tank Corps, AEF, and shortly thereafter was placed on General Pershing's staff as an adviser on all tank matters. On

January 26, 1918, assembly of the Tank Corps began. Its authorized strength was 14,827. The light tank service was to organize in France, the heavy tank service in England. The light tank service was commanded by Lt-Col. George S. Patton Jr. and started with 22 second lieutenants transferred from the Coast Artillery. The heavy tank service, commanded by Lt-Col. Conrad S. Babcock, began with 58 unassigned Engineer Reserve Officers and 38 enlisted men.

Theoretically, according to the tables of organization and equipment (TOE), a light tank battalion was to consist of 72 light tanks and a heavy tank battalion of 69 heavy tanks. In both types of battalion there were to be three companies of three platoons, each platoon with five tanks, and a company HQ. A tank brigade was to have two light battalions, a heavy battalion, a repair and salvage company, and a brigade HQ.

The United States Tank Corps—and it is unnecessary to add the words "in World War I" because the designation was abolished in 1920 and has never been resurrected —the U.S. Tank Corps was organized in two distinct parts. While this dichotomy is understandable from the operational and organizational points of view it gives rise to some confusion unless the explanation is taken in some detail.

The two parts were: the Tank Corps, American Expeditionary Forces (Tank Corps AEF); and the stateside Tank Service, National Army (as it was originally called). Authority for the Tank Service, National Army was given on February 18, 1918— twenty-three days after the Tank Corps, AEF, began assembling. It was authorized under the Chief of Engineers. Three weeks later, on March 5, by which time organization of the first tank units had started, the Engineers shed their tutelage and the Tank Service, National Army, became a separate branch. Seventeen days after that, March 22, the Tank Service, National Army, was re-designated the Tank Corps, National Army. There was thus now a Tank Corps, AEF, in France and England, and a Tank Corps, National Army, in the United States.

The first director of the Tank Corps, National Army, was Colonel Ira C. Welborn. His duties were to organize, arm, equip and train tank units in the United States, and he was responsible for all tank activities there. The authorized strength of the Tank Corps, National Army, was slightly greater than that of the Tank Corps, AEF— 914 officers and 14,746 men. The primary tank training camp in the United States was Camp Colt, Pennsylvania, whose commander during some seven months of 1918 was Dwight D. Eisenhower. During the course of this command Eisenhower was promoted from Captain to Lieutenant-Colonel, and while he welcomed this promotion his satisfaction was nevertheless tinged with regret because it meant that he was not allowed to take the first U.S. tank unit overseas—in fact he had got as far as the New York docks in command of this unit when he was hauled back to run Camp Colt.

While there was an ultimate relationship between the two Tank Corps in that the Tank Corps, National Army, was raising and training units for action on the Western Front in the Tank Corps, AEF, there was no direct command relationship between them. Among other complications this diarchy initially gave rise to duplication in unit designations. But this duplication was soon eliminated and all tank units in both Tank Corps were re-numbered, without repetition, in the 300 series from 301 through 346. Of these, however, only 301 through 308, and 326 through 346 were organized.

The first tank units in the Tank Service (later Corps), National Army, were constituted and organized in February 1918 as elements of the 65th Engineers. Companies A, B, and C of the 1st Separate Battalion, Heavy Tank Service, 65th Engineers, and the 1st and 2nd Battalions, Light Tank Service, 65th Engineers were organized at Camp Upton, New York; and Company D, 2nd Battalion, Heavy Tank Service, 65th Engineers was organized at Camp Meade, Maryland. On March 16, the designation of the 1st Separate Battalion was changed to 1st Heavy Battalion, Tank Service, and on April 16, with Captain Eisenhower in command, it was changed yet again to 41st Heavy Battalion, Tank Corps. The battalion was now transferred to England—leaving its commanding officer reluctantly behind to take over Camp Colt—and on April 25 it received its last change of designation in World War I and became 301st Battalion, Tank Corps, AEF. It had arrived at the Tank Corps, AEF, Tank Center in England, and from there four months later went to France under the command of Major Roger B. Harrison.

Eight Tank Centers were organized, six in the United States (numbered 303rd, 304th, 309th, 310th, 311th, and 314th), and two in Europe. The first of these two to be organized was set up in February 1918 at Bovington Camp, near Wareham, Dorset, in England. Bovington was the home of the British Tank Corps, and the personnel of the new Tank Center were trained in the Bovington tank schools. The other Tank Center of the Tank Corps, AEF, was organized in March 1918 at Bourg, in France. The Bourg center was designated the 1st Light Tank Center, and the center at Bovington was designated the 2nd Heavy Tank Center. Later these were re-designated the 301st and 302nd Tank Centers respectively.

Four tank brigades were formed. Initially organized as the 1st, 2nd, 3rd, and 4th Provisional Brigades, Tank Corps, their designations were changed just before the Armistice to the 304th, 305th, 306th, and 307th Brigades, Tank Corps.

Only four battalions of the Tank Corps saw action. Three of them were light battalions equipped with French Renault F.T. tanks (F.T.=Faible Tonnage=light weight), one was a heavy battalion equipped with British Mark V and Mark V Star tanks. The heavy battalion was the 301st, whose lineage we have already traced, the light battalions were the 331st, the 344th, and the 345th.

Of these three light battalions the brunt of the fighting was taken by the 344th and the 345th, which were the first American tank units in action, while the 331st only joined the AEF a few days before the Armistice on November 11, 1918. The lineage of the 344th and the 345th was as follows:

Until September 12, 1918, the day on which American tank units first entered combat, the battalions were respectively designated the 326th and 327th. Company A of the 326th was re-designated on June 6 from Company A, Tank Service Detachment, AEF, which was constituted on April 25 and organized in France. Company B of the 326th was re-designated on September 1 from Company B, 1st Tank Center, AEF in France, which had been organized on April 16 from Provisional Company B, Tank Service—itself organized on February 17, the

The 6-Ton Radio tank of 1920 was a copy of the corresponding French Renault Char TSF.   (Courtesy Armin Sohns)

day before the Tank Service was actually authorized. Company C was re-designated on June 6 from Company C, 1st Battalion, Tank Center, which was constituted on April 25 (an important date, it will be noticed, in the formation of the United States Tank Corps) and organized in England.

The lineage of the 327th Battalion was considerably simpler than that of the 326th. It was organized in France on June 7, and was re-designated the 344th Battalion on September 12.

The combat debut of the 344th and 345th Battalions on September 12, 1918, was in an attack against the St. Mihiel salient to the south of Verdun. The two battalions were in the 1st Provisional (later the 304th) Brigade, Tank Corps, which was commanded by Lieutenant-Colonel George S. Patton, Jr., under whom they had trained. The brigade was organized at Langres, Haute Marne. Each battalion had 45 French Renaults, with 16 tanks from the 344th and 25 from the 345th in the brigade reserve. The 344th was assigned to the 1st Division, the 345th to the 42nd.

From then on these two battalions were in almost continuous action during the Meuse-Argonne campaign. Their shortage of tanks became such that General Pershing sent Rockenbach to Paris with instructions "to give anything in the AEF for 500 tanks." But only 48 could be obtained.

Patton covered himself in glory at Saint-Mihiel at the head of a tank battalion, urging his armor on in a way

that only those who have been privileged to serve under him can truly appreciate. And he had done this, not, it will surprise none who knew him to learn, according to the canon of the time which decreed that tanks should operate only in support of infantry, but, as the French so graphically put it, "en fer de lance." Not long afterwards, however, on September 26 in the Argonne forest he was wounded while directing his tanks against enemy machine-gun nests. Fortunately for the Allies in World War II he recovered—only to lose his life by an unfortunate accident in post-war Germany. For the remainder of the Meuse-Argonne campaign the light tank brigade was commanded by Major Sereno Brett.

The 301st Battalion, as mentioned earlier, arrived in France towards the end of August 1918, the first, and as it turned out, the only battalion in the 2nd Provisional (later the 305th) Brigade, Tank Corps. Having been trained on British tanks at Bovington the 301st was to remain with the British Tank Corps until it could be equipped with American-built tanks. None were available when it arrived in France, so it was equipped with 47 British Mark Vs and Mark V Stars and attached to the British IV Tank Brigade. The brigade was employed in support of the American II Corps, consisting of the 27th and 30th U.S. Divisions, and the Australian Corps in Fourth British Army during the Storming of the Hindenburg Line at the end of September 1918. The 301st first went into action with the 27th Division on September 29 between Cambrai and St. Quentin in the Battle of Le

7

Catelet-Bony. It had a grim start. Many of the tanks were knocked out and others were wrecked by running on to an old British minefield, a forgotten relic from an earlier battle.

The 301st's next action was on October 8 at Brancourt with the 30th Division, when only ten of its twenty tanks rallied after gaining the final objective. On the 17th it supported both divisions of American II Corps in the Battle of the Selle, and six days later fought its last action in support of two British divisions near Bazuel in the Marmol Forest. By this time its strength was down to barely a dozen tanks.

On November 11, 1918 the war ended. The Tank Corps, AEF, was practically without tanks. But, together with the Tank Corps, National Army, it had 1,090 officers and 14,780 men, of whom about half were in the United States and the other half in France or en route.

II
(1919–1940)

Unlike its British counterpart the American Tank Corps did not long survive the war. General Staff plans for a Tank Corps of five tank brigades and a GHQ, based on a reorganized Regular Army of five corps, each of four divisions, were cancelled by the National Defense Act of 1920, which created the Army of the United States, consisting of the Regular Army, the Organized Reserves, and the National Guard. The 1920 Act abolished the Tank Corps. Tanks were no longer an independent arm. Formalizing the support rôle that had been predominant in World War I experience the Act laid down that henceforward all tank units were to form a part of the infantry and were to be known as "Infantry (Tanks)."

Translated into terms of unit assignment this meant primarily one tank company allotted to each infantry and cavalry division, a total of thirteen separate companies (numbered the 1st through the 13th) of which, in practice, only ten were actually organized. There were also five tank battalions (numbered the 15th through the 19th, of which all but the last were activated) and the HQ, 1st Tank Group. The Tank Group HQ and the four active battalions all traced their origins to Tank Corps organizations of World War I.

On September 1, 1929, the five battalions and the Tank Group HQ were formed into the 1st and 2nd Tank Regiments. Three years later, in October 1932, these were re-designated respectively the 66th Infantry (Light Tanks) and the 67th Infantry (Medium Tanks). The following year two new light tank regiments were constituted, the 68th and 69th. At the beginning of 1940 the 68th was organized from some of the divisional tank companies, but the 69th was disbanded without ever being activated. Soon after the 68th was organized it joined the 66th and 67th in forming the Provisional Tank Brigade at Fort Benning, Georgia. The brigade was commanded by Colonel Bruce Magruder.

1st Tank Regiment On September 1, 1929, the 1st Tank Regiment was organized. HQ and HQ Company were a re-designation of HQ and HQ Company 1st Tank Group, which itself had been formed on June 22, 1921 by the consolidation and re-designation of HQ and HQ Companies of 304th and 305th Tank Brigades, Tank Corps. The remainder of 1st Tank Regiment was organized by the re-designation of the following existing units: 16th Tank Battalion as 1st Battalion, 15th Tank Battalion as 2nd Battalion, 18th Battalion as 3rd Battalion, and 21st Tank Maintenance Company as Service Company.

All these units had their origins in tank organizations of World War I. All had first appeared in 1918: 16th

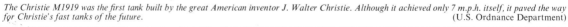

The Christie M1919 was the first tank built by the great American inventor J. Walter Christie. Although it achieved only 7 m.p.h. itself, it paved the way for Christie's fast tanks of the future. (U.S. Ordnance Department)

As well as tanks J. Walter Christie also designed self-propelled weapons. His first was the M1916 SP 3 in. AA gun carriage. In 1923 came the model seen here: Wheeled Caterpillar Christie for 4.7 in. AA gun. The driver sat in the rear. (U.S. Ordnance Department)

The Mark VI M1 105-mm Self-Propelled Howitzer of 1926 was one of many SPs offered by the U.S. Ordnance Department but rejected by the Field Artillery. (Infantry Journal)

Light tanks were originally carried on trucks for road moves in order to increase track life. A 6-Ton tank of the 6th Tank Company demonstrating de-trucking without a ramp in 1927. (Col. R. J. Icks)

The 23-ton medium tank of 1926 was developed from the earlier Medium A or M1921 and the Medium M1922. It was designated Medium T1. It appeared at a time when the Infantry, having in 1924 decided that it wanted only medium tanks, reversed that decision and now opted for light tanks only. Although the Infantry were the sole users of tanks, medium tank development nevertheless continued. (U.S. Army SC92989)

Tank Battalion as HQ and HQ Company, 327th Battalion, Tank Corps, and Company C, 1st Separate Battalion, Heavy Tank Service, 65th Engineers; 15th Tank Battalion as elements of the 1st Battalion, Tank Center (organized in England), and Company A, 1st Separate Battalion, Heavy Tank Service, 65th Engineers; 18th Tank Battalion as 329th Battalion, Tank Corps, and HQ and HQ Company, 328th Battalion, Tank Corps; 21st Maintenance Company as 316th Repair and Salvage Company, Tank Corps.

The 1st Tank Regiment was itself converted, re-organized and re-designated on October 25, 1932 as 66th Infantry (Light Tanks). 66th Infantry in turn, on July 15, 1940, became 66th Armored Regiment and was assigned to 2nd Armored Division with which it served until March 25, 1946.

2nd Tank Regiment The regiment was organized with only one active battalion, its 2nd, which was a re-designation of the 17th Tank Battalion. The rest of the regiment—all inactive—were a newly constituted HQ and HQ Company, a newly constituted 3rd Battalion, and a 1st Battalion which was a re-designated 19th Tank Battalion, which itself had been constituted in the Regular Army on March 24, 1923, but had remained inactive. The 17th Tank Battalion, however, gave the 2nd Tank Regiment a link with the Tank Corps for, through some of its personnel, it could trace its origins to 1918 when it was organized as the 303rd Battalion and as elements of the 1st Separate Battalion, Heavy Tank Service, 65th Engineers.

The 2nd Tank Regiment was re-designated on October 31, 1932 as 67th Infantry (Medium Tanks). 67th Infantry in turn, on July 15, 1940, was re-organized and re-designated 67th Armored Regiment and was assigned to 2nd Armored Division with which it served until March 25, 1946.

Organized Reserves and National Guard Each division of the Organized Reserves, severely under-strength though

they all were, had a tank company. These companies were numbered the 76th through the 91st, the 94th through the 104th, and the 461st through the 466th. Following the Regular Army pattern, tank battalions and HQs of Tank Groups were also organized. The tank battalions were numbered the 301st through the 324th, and the HQs of Tank Groups the 6th through the 12th. Three of the tank battalions (the 301st, the 306th, and the 314th) were disbanded in 1928, and the following year the remainder—once again following the Regular Army pattern as set by the 1st and 2nd Tank Regiments— were reorganized as elements of the 306th through the 312th Tank Regiments. In 1932, when the 1st and 2nd Tank Regiments became the 66th Infantry (Light Tanks) and the 67th Infantry (Medium Tanks), the Tank Regiments of the Organized Reserves were re-designated as the 420th Infantry (Tanks) through the 426th Infantry (Tanks). In 1933 the 427th Infantry (Tanks) was organized.

Tank companies were also organized for the National Guard's divisions. These companies were numbered the 22nd through the 24th, the 26th through the 38th, and the 40th through the 45th. Unlike the Regular Army and the Organized Reserves the National Guard had no tank battalions as such until World War II when some of the divisional tank companies having been called into Federal service were used to form four tank battalions, the 191st through the 194th.

THE MECHANIZED FORCE

The abolition of the Tank Corps as an independent arm under the provisions of the 1920 National Defense Act did not abolish the development of armored theory in private among those infantry and cavalry officers who were convinced of the critical necessity for an armored force acting as an entity instead of simply as a support for infantry. This line of thought was typical of its time among military thinkers of the same stamp in other countries, especially in Britain and Germany.

The Infantry's decision in 1926 to use only light tanks resulted in the Light T1 tank series, which was produced in collaboration with the Society of Automotive Engineers. The Light Tank T1E2, seen here, appeared in 1929. Like the previous models in the series it had its engine in front and had a 37-mm gun as its main armament.
(U.S. Ordnance Department)

75-mm Howitzer Motor Carriage T1 of the 1930 period with weapon at maximum elevation. (U.S. Ordnance Department)

It was in Britain that the iconoclasts broke through, despite powerful opposition from "the old and bold". The pressures of the armored enthusiasts resulted in the formation in 1927 of an Experimental Mechanized Force composed of armored cars, tankettes, tanks, a motorized machine-gun battalion, field artillery which was tractor-towed or self-propelled, and motorized engineers. A truck-borne infantry battalion was attached for most of the Force's exercises, and air support (reconnaissance, fighter, and bomber) was also provided. The following year the name of the Force was changed to Experimental Armored Force and its maneuvers were devoted more to functional practice than to organizational experiment as they had been the previous year. Present as an observer at the 1927 maneuvers was Dwight F. Davis, the United States Secretary of War. He was so impressed by what he saw and by what the maneuvers so clearly presaged that

on his return to the States he directed that a similar force be developed in the U.S. Army.

The experimental mechanized force resulting from this directive was assembled at Camp Meade, Maryland, from July 1 to September 20, 1928. It consisted of elements from the Infantry, including Infantry (Tanks), the Cavalry, Field Artillery, Air Corps, Engineers, Ordnance, Chemical Warfare Service, and the Medical Corps. Although insufficient funds and obsolete equipment prevented the re-assembly of the force the following year, its few weeks of activity were not nugatory because the War Department Mechanization Board, which had been appointed to study the experiment, recommended that a mechanized force be permanently established. This recommendation was acted upon by the Army Chief of Staff, General Charles P. Summerall, who, on the eve of leaving office in October 1930, directed that a

The M1 Armored Car was the first U.S. armored car to be designed as such. (Col. R. J. Icks)

The Cavalry's T5 Armored Car (also known as the Combat Car T2 Modified) of 1931 was both a half-track and a wheeled vehicle.
(U.S. Ordnance Department)

Communications car model of the T9 Scout Car in use by the Communications Officer of the 1st Cavalry, Mechanized.
(Post Studio, Fort Knox)

permanent mechanized force be assembled immediately and stationed at Fort Eustis, Virginia.

The Mechanized Force was organized under the command of Colonel Daniel Van Voorhis, who thus earned for himself in later years the title of "Grandfather of the Armored Force". But the "permanency" was short-lived. In 1931 the new Army Chief of Staff, General Douglas MacArthur, decided that instead of mechanization being the prerogative of a separate force—apart, that is, from the 1st and 2nd Tank Regiments and the divisional tank companies which were part of the infantry—all arms and services were to adopt mechanization and motorization "as far as is practicable and desirable." To this end all arms and services were allowed to experiment with armor and mechanization, and the separate Mechanized Force at Fort Eustis was dissolved. But lest anyone might see in this new directive the opening of the door on the possibility of re-forming a separate Tank Corps in the future, General MacArthur stated unequivocally that no separate corps would be established "in the vain hope that through a utilization of machines it can absorb the missions, and duplicate the capabilities of all others." Although tanks were no longer to be the preserve of the infantry there was no question of them regaining their World War I autonomy.

The arm that benefited most from the 1931 directive was the cavalry. This was not a view that all cavalry officers would have agreed with. As in Britain and Germany the development of the tank mechanically and its growing importance both strategically and tactically—albeit this was confined to discussions and exercises—reinforced the antagonism of the older combat arms which equated the rise of the tank with their own decline in importance, and therefore in financial appropriations. With only a meagre amount allotted for national defense as a whole, newcomers were not welcome. On top of this as far as the "old and bold" in the cavalry were concerned was the love for the horse and the disgust for things mechanical. Read the comments of senior cavalry officers in any country and they might be carbon copies of the same speech. It was not unnatural.

But the more far-seeing realised that without mechanization the cavalry was likely to be out of business. They did not agree with those who maintained that the lack of opportunity for the cavalry on the Western Front in 1914–1918 was the exception rather than the rule. They argued that although the traditional cavalry missions had not altered, the horse was no longer the right mount on which to carry them out. That the airplane would take over the very long range reconnaissance mission from the cavalry was common ground between them and the unyielding horse-lovers. What was at issue was whether the machine should replace the horse for other cavalry missions—protecting flanks, covering advance or retreat, medium range reconnaissance, pursuit. Those who favored the retention of the horse could point to the slowness of the tanks available; but as speeds and reliability increased this argument faltered. Even by the late 1920s a few light armored vehicles were in use in cavalry units, and the 1931 directive encouraged this acceptance. The interest of the cavalry, wrote General MacArthur, was now "centered on armored cars and cross-country vehicles possessing a high degree of strategic mobility, with fighting and tactical mobility an important though secondary consideration." Cavalry was therefore instructed to develop combat vehicles which would "enhance its power in rôles of reconnaissance, counter-reconnaissance, flank action, pursuit, and similar operations." One cavalry regiment was to lose its horses and be equipped exclusively with these new vehicles. The infantry, meanwhile, was to concentrate on developing tanks which could more effectively support the rifleman in dislodging the enemy from strongly held positions.

The "horses only" school had a further set-back in 1933 when General MacArthur pointed out that "the horse has no higher degree of mobility today than he had a thousand years ago. The time has therefore arrived when the Cavalry arm must either replace or assist the horse as a means of transportation, or else pass into the limbo of discarded military formations." This did not mean, however, that the tasks of the cavalry were outmoded. There would always be "the need for certain units capable of performing more distant missions than can be efficiently carried out by the mass of the Army. The elements assigned to these tasks will be the cavalry of the future, but manifestly the horse alone will not meet its requirements in transportation."

After such a dictum, the percipient realized, complete mechanization of the cavalry was now a cloud somewhat larger than a man's hand.

The cavalry at this period consisted of fourteen regiments—the 1st through the 14th Cavalry—and a regiment of Philippine Scouts, the 26th Cavalry, which was organized in 1922. In addition there were 18 cavalry regiments in the National Guard and 24 in the Organized Reserves. At the end of World War I there had been seventeen cavalry regiments in the Regular Army. In order to meet the requirements of the 1920 National Defense Act three regiments—the 15th, 16th, and 17th—were inactivated and the remainder were re-organized to consist of HQ, HQ troop, service troop, and six lettered troops (i.e. Troop A through Troop F in two squadrons of three troops each), instead of 12 lettered troops and a machine-gun troop in addition to the HQ, HQ troop, and supply troop (as the service troop was previously called). Some separate machine-gun troops and machine-gun squadrons were organized in place of the regimental machine-gun troops. The loss to the cavalry arm by this post-war reduction was three complete regiments and 98 troops, "some of the troops," as the official history points out, "having been in continuous existence for almost a hundred years."*

Further major changes in the cavalry were made in 1928 when the number of lettered troops was reduced to four (divided between two squadrons) and the separate machine-gun squadrons and troops were eliminated, each regiment now having its own machine-gun troop again.

Having received its orders to develop combat vehicles the cavalry selected Fort Knox, Kentucky, as the location for its task. The nucleus of the command was formed by personnel and equipment from the Mechanized Force at Fort Eustis, so that in effect it can be said that that Force never ceased to exist and there is a continuity, admittedly a little wobbly in 1929, that ran from the experimental mechanized force of 1928 to the formation of the first armored divisions in 1940—just as in Britain there is a continuity, also somewhat limping in its early stages, between the Experimental Mechanized Force of 1927 and the formation of the first armored division, known originally as the Mobile Division, in 1938.

The regiment selected to lead the van of mechanization was the 1st Cavalry. It arrived at Fort Knox from Marfa, Texas, early in 1933, and began to replace its horses by AFVs. The organization of the mechanized regiment was similar to that of a horse regiment. It had four lettered troops, two of them in a covering squadron, one being an armored car troop, the other a scout troop, and two in a combat car squadron, both of them being combat car troops. The regiment had 35 light tanks which were about equally divided between the scout troop and the two combat car troops. The term "combat car" was invented to overcome the restriction of the 1920 National Defense Act which laid down that only the infantry were to have tanks and that all tank units were to be part of the infantry. Thus it was a case of "a tank by any other name" for the track-laying fighting vehicles used by the cavalry, and the other name chosen was "combat car". But it was the name only that differed, apart from one other feature. In order to economize, the light tank design that was evolved in 1933 was adaptable for both infantry and cavalry. It could support the infantry, in theory at least, in dislodging the enemy from strong defensive positions; and it could meet the needs of the cavalry in its pursuit, protection, and reconnaissance rôles. This new tank, the T2, could achieve a top speed of 35 m.p.h. In its T2E1 and T2E2 versions it had fixed turrets—a single turret in the case of the T2E1 and twin turrets side by side in the case of the T2E2—and was intended for the infantry support rôle. In its T2E3 version, which was identical in all other respects to the T2E1, it had a simple hand-traversed fully rotating turret for the cavalry rôle. The T2E1 was standardized as the Light Tank M2A1, and the T2E3 was standardized as the Combat Car M1.

Over the next few years several other units including the 13th Cavalry, a field artillery battalion, and a quartermaster company, were moved to Fort Knox and there mechanized. And the cavalry division itself received an armored car troop, a tank company, and an air observation squadron. Early in 1938 a modification was made to the 1931 directive: mechanization would in future no longer be developed by all arms but only by the infantry and the cavalry. The Fort Knox units were formed into the 7th Cavalry Brigade (Mechanized), with Brigadier General Van Voorhis in command. Later in the year he was succeeded by Colonel Adna R.

---

* Army Lineage Series, op. cit. p. 53. It is interesting to note that in 1922 the British Cavalry lost eight of its thirty regiments by amalgamation.

The turretless Light Tank T3 of 1936 was a product of the financially lean years. The driver sat on the left and there was a machine-gun sponson on the right glacis. (U.S. Ordnance Department)

Combat Car M1A1 used by the 7th Cavalry Brigade (Mechanized) was fast and agile. Built in 1937 it had its turret off-set to the left, was equipped with radio, and weighed 9·75 tons. This particular vehicle belonged to the 1st Cavalry, Mechanized. (Post Studio, Fort Knox)

The Combat Car T5E1 of 1935 was built during the period of interest in a barbette type of superstructure. (U.S. Ordnance Department)

Chaffee, a strong advocate of armor, who had been second-in-command of the Mechanized Force at Fort Eustis. Chaffee was known, with justice, as the "Father of the Armored Force".

The armor enthusiasts now began to press more openly for the formation of complete armored divisions, initially by the expansion of the 7th Cavalry Brigade (Mechanized) into a division. The United States, they could point out, was in danger of falling critically behind in respect of an armored force. The German panzer divisions had already begun to hint at their power in maneuvers and in the occupation of Austria and Czechoslovakia. The British had at last listened to the arguments of their own tank experts and had formed an armored division. But although the Chiefs of Infantry and Cavalry, the two arms now exclusively concerned with mechanization, were agreeable in principle to the proposal neither was prepared to release units for conversion. Nevertheless an *ad hoc* armored division was improvised for the 1940 maneuvers in Louisiana. The 6th Infantry, a motorized regiment, was added to Chaffee's 7th Cavalry Brigade (Mechanized), and the

brigade combined with Bruce Magruder's Provisional Tank Brigade—with devastating effect!

The sands of opposition were fast running out. The action of the 7th Cavalry Brigade in the 1939 maneuvers along the Champlain Valley near Plattsburgh, the rapid overwhelming of Poland by the German panzer divisions, the domination of the 1940 maneuvers in Louisiana by the mechanized forces, and the apocalyptic success of the panzer divisions in the Low Countries and France, all combined to lend irrefutable urgency to the argument of Chaffee and the other armor leaders that mechanization was not proceeding swiftly enough under the aegis of the infantry and the cavalry, and that there must immediately be created an armored force which would be free from the control of other arms and which would, as rapidly as possible, organize the U.S. Army's own panzer divisions.

On July 10, 1940, the Armored Force was created with Brigadier General Adna R. Chaffee as its first chief. Because there was no Congressional authorization for a separate armored branch of the Army it was established "for purposes of service test."

The M2A3 Light Tank of 1938, like the M2A2 and the T2E2 from which the latter was standardized, copied the dual turret layout of the Vickers 6-Ton tank. The left turret was octagonal, the right cylindrical.
(Courtesy Col. G. B. Jarrett)

Convertible Combat Car T7 of 1938 was the last of the Christie type vehicles built in the United States. (U.S. Ordnance Department)

15

M2A4 Light Tank, with its single manually-traversed turret mounting a 37-mm gun as its main armament, during the 1940 maneuvers in Louisiana. The M2A4 also had a co-axial ·30 Browning machine-gun, and four other weapons of this caliber: in the bow, on a pintle at the turret rear for AA fire, and two forward-firing (one in each side sponson). Four of the six weapons can be seen in this photograph. It was at the 1940 maneuvers that the ad hoc armored division dominated the scene. On July 10, 1940 the Armored Force was created. (Courtesy T. C. Lopez)

III
(1940–1945)

The Armored Force, with Brigadier General Adna R. Chaffee as its chief, was created on July 10, 1940. Five days later, under the new Armored Force, I Armored Corps was activated. This consisted of the 1st and 2nd Armored Divisions, both of which were activated on that same day, July 15, 1940, the 1st at Fort Knox, Kentucky, the 2nd at Fort Benning, Georgia.

As well as its two armored divisions the new Armored Force had one separate or non-divisional tank battalion, the 70th Tank Battalion, which was constituted in the Regular Army on July 15, 1940, and activated at Fort Meade, Maryland. It also had an Armored Force Board, and an Armored Force School and Replacement Training Center.

The 1st Armored Division was the successor to the 7th Cavalry Brigade (Mechanized). The two cavalry regiments in the 7th Cavalry Brigade—the 1st Cavalry Mechanized and the 13th Cavalry Mechanized—were re-organized and re-designated respectively the 1st Armored Regiment and the 13th Armored Regiment, and both were assigned to the 1st Armored Division.

THE ARMORED DIVISIONS

The organization of a U.S. armored division at this time contained all the elements present in German and British armored divisions: command, reconnaissance, strike, support, and service. The strike element, tanks, was as greatly accentuated in the American armored division as in its British and German counterparts. Compared with the German panzer division's tanks, which propaganda made out to be 416 but which in practice varied from 146 to 292 at the time of the *blitzkrieg* against the Low Countries and France in May–June 1940, (and it should be remembered that by far the greater number of these were the Panzer I and Panzer II and ex-Czech 35(t) and 38(t) light tanks), the British armored division had 337 tanks and the American armored division had 368. And here a reminder must be added: these were paper figures only. The Armored Force came into being with only a few hundred light tanks to its name. Not until 1943 was the huge might of American industry running in top gear and the equipment shortage beginning to be overcome, and by then tactical and logistical experience had dictated that the number of tanks in an armored division be considerably reduced.

The tanks in the original U.S. armored division organization were in an armored brigade consisting of

Marmon-Herrington CTLS-4TAC and CTLS-4TAY Light Tanks in Alaska. The 4TAC had a left-hand turret, the 4TAY had a right-hand turret. Both mounted a ·30 cal. machine-gun, and both tanks weighed 8·4 tons. These tanks were built on a commercial order for the Netherlands East Indies but could not be delivered because of the Japanese conquest of those islands in 1942. Some were taken over by the U.S. Army, their U.S. designations being T14 for the 4TAC (in foreground) and T16 for the 4TAY (in background). (Courtesy Marmon-Herrington Co.)

The so-called Trackless Tank of 1940 was a commercial venture by the Trackless Tank Corporation of New York which later was produced as the T13 Armored Car. (U.S. Ordnance Department)

M3A1 Medium tank of 31st Armored Regiment, 7th Armored Division, in trouble during maneuvers in Louisiana, October 1942. The M3A1 (Lee Mark II to the British) had a cast hull. This is a later vehicle in which the side doors have been eliminated. The M3 Medium was an interim vehicle but it proved its worth at a critical stage in the Allies' fortunes. (U.S. Army SC147198)

three armored regiments, two light and one medium, and a field artillery regiment of two battalions. The 1st and the 13th were the two light armored regiments in the 1st Armored Division; the medium armored regiment was created by constituting a new 69th Armored Regiment on July 15, 1940, and activating it at Fort Knox on July 31.

For reconnaissance the armored division had an armored reconnaissance battalion and an attached air observation squadron. In the case of 1st Armored Division the former was the 1st Reconnaissance Battalion (Armored) which had been constituted in the Regular Army on April 22, 1940 as 7th Reconnaissance and Support Squadron (Mechanized), activated at Fort Knox on June 1, and re-organized and re-designated on July 15, the day it was assigned to 1st Armored Division.

The support element had an armored infantry regiment, a field artillery battalion, and an engineer battalion. In 1st Armored Division these were 6th Infantry (Armored), 27th Field Artillery Battalion (Armored), and 16th Engineer Battalion (Armored).

The services were a signals company, a maintenance company, a quartermaster truck battalion, and a medical battalion.

The 2nd Armored Division was organized from the Provisional Tank Brigade at Fort Benning, the brigade consisting of approximately seven infantry tank battalions in the three Infantry (Tanks) regiments, the 66th, 67th, and 68th. On July 15, 1940 these three were designated as the 66th, 67th, and 68th Armored Regiment. The division's armored reconnaissance battalion was the 2nd Reconnaissance Battalion (Armored) which was also constituted on July 15. Its infantry regiment was the 41st Infantry (Armored).

"Heavy" Armored Divisions During the course of World War II the U.S. armored division—as was also the case

with the British and German armored divisions—was reorganized several times in the light of tactical, logistical, and other experience. There were five reorganizations in the U.S. armored division in all. But only two need be considered as of major importance.

The first major re-organization was ordered on March 1, 1942. It resulted in what was called the "heavy" armored division. The armored brigade organization disappeared and along with it one of the armored regiments, leaving in place of the brigade set-up two Combat Commands, popularly known as CCA and CCB, and two armored regiments. Each of these armored regiments has three tank battalions but the proportion of light and medium tanks was changed, there now being two medium battalions to one light battalion in each regiment.

Artillery was also re-organized. There were now three identical artillery regiments under a divisional artillery commander instead of two battalions in an artillery regiment in the armored brigade and one battalion in the division's support element.

The introduction of Combat Commands gave the division great flexibility because, while they remained as permanent and experienced headquarters with staff who were used to working together, the divisional units under their command could be composed of any "mix" that the divisional commander considered necessary for the mission in hand, and that "mix" could remain unchanged for as long or as short a time as he considered desirable.

By the time this first major re-organization was ordered the Armored Force was expanding enormously. Six armored divisions had been activated and were in various stages of training or formation, ranging from the 1st and 2nd which were almost ready for combat to the 6th which dated only from February 1942. There had also been an increase in the number of separate tank battalions.

The M3A1 Scout Car with tarpaulin top in place. These vehicles, of which over 20,000 were built during World War II, were the pre-war M3 Scout Cars with a wider hull and a sprung roller in place of a front bumper. (U.S. Ordnance Department)

75-mm M3 Self-Propelled Gun used by the Tank Destroyer Force in North Africa in 1943. This weapon was developed under the direction of Major (later Colonel) Robert J. Icks.

(U.S. Army 1312 Ord 151)

As far as the armored divisions' strike element was concerned the result of the March 1, 1942 re-organization, was that the 1st Armored Division shed the 69th Armored Regiment, which had been assigned to the 6th Armored Division on February 15, and the 2nd Armored Division shed the 68th Armored Regiment which had also been assigned to the 6th Armored Division on the same date.

The 3rd Armored Division, activated at Camp Beauregard, Louisiana, on April 15, 1941, with the 2nd, 3rd, and 4th Armored Regiments (all three of which were constituted in the Regular Army on January 13, 1941, and had no previous origins) and which on May 8, 1941 were re-designated the 32nd, 33rd, and 40th Armored Regiments, shed the 40th Armored Regiment which was assigned to the 7th Armored Division on March 2, 1942.

The 4th Armored Division, activated at Pine Camp, New York, on April 15, 1941, had the 35th and 37th Armored Regiments, which had been constituted in the Regular Army on January 13, 1941 as the 5th and 7th Armored Regiments and re-designated on May 8, 1941.

The 5th Armored Division, activated at Fort Knox, Kentucky, on October 1, 1941 had the 34th and 81st Armored Regiments which were constituted in the Regular Army on August 28, 1941, and activated on October 1, 1941.

The 6th Armored Division, activated at Fort Knox, Kentucky, on February 15, 1941, had the 68th Armored Regiment from the 2nd Armored Division and the 69th Armored Regiment from the 1st Armored Division, as mentioned above.

By late 1942, eight more armored divisions had been activated, and in 1943 two more, making a total of sixteen in all. These sixteen all saw service against the European Axis powers, none was used in the Pacific theater against the Japanese.

The date and location of activation, the campaigns in which each served, and the nickname which each division acquired, are as follows:

Armd. Div.	Date and Location of activation	Nickname	Campaigns
1st	July 15, 1940 at Fort Knox, Kentucky	Old Ironsides	North Africa (Tunisia), Italy
2nd	July 15, 1940 at Fort Benning, Georgia	Hell on Wheels	North Africa (Algeria, French Morocco), Sicily, North-West Europe 1, 2, 3, 4, 5
3rd	April 15, 1941 at Camp Beauregard, Louisiana	Spearhead	North-West Europe 1, 2, 3, 4, 5
4th	April 15, 1941 at Pine Camp, New York	None—"4th Armored" was name enough. But occasionally called Breakthrough	North-West Europe 1, 2, 3, 4, 5
5th	October 1, 1941 at Fort Knox, Kentucky	Victory	North-West Europe 1, 2, 3, 4, 5
6th	February 15, 1942 at Fort Knox, Kentucky	Super Sixth	North-West Europe 1, 2, 3, 4, 5
7th	March 1, 1942 at Camp Polk, Louisiana	Lucky Seventh	North-West Europe 1, 2, 3, 4, 5
8th	April 1, 1942 at Fort Knox, Kentucky as a training cadre: became a combat division in February 1943	Originally Iron Snake, then Thundering Herd, and finally Tornado	North-West Europe 2, 3, 4, 5
9th	July 15, 1942 at Fort Riley, Kansas	Phantom	North-West Europe 2, 3, 4, 5
10th	July 15, 1942 at Fort Benning, Georgia	Tiger	North-West Europe 2, 3, 4, 5
11th	August 15, 1942 at Camp Polk, Louisiana	Thunderbolt	North-West Europe 3, 4, 5
12th	September 15, 1942 at Camp Campbell, Kentucky	Hellcat	North-West Europe 3, 4, 5
13th	October 15, 1942 at Camp Beale, California	Black Cat	North-West Europe 3, 4, 5
14th	November 15, 1942 at Camp Chaffee, Arkansas	Liberator	North-West Europe 3, 4, 5
16th	July 15, 1943 at Camp Chaffee, Arkansas	None	North-West Europe 3, 5
20th	March 15, 1943 at Camp Campbell, Kentucky	None	North-West Europe 3, 5

NOTE: North-West Europe=the campaign that began in Normandy, France, on June 6, 1944. For official Campaign Participation Credits it is divided up into (1) Normandy (2) Northern France (3) Rhineland (4) Ardennes-Alsace (5) Central Europe.

M3 Light tanks of 70th Tank Battalion training in Iceland, April 1942.

(U.S. Army 137628)

"Light" Armored Divisions The first major re-organization resulted in what were called "heavy" divisions. The second major re-organization, which was ordered on September 15, 1943, turned the armored divisions into what were called "light" divisions. The main difference between the heavy and the light armored division was a further reduction in the division's tank strength by replacing the two armored regiments (a total of six tank battalions) with three tank battalions. Except in the case of the 2nd and 3rd Armored Divisions, to which the 1943 re-organization was not applied, the regimental organization was abolished. The armored infantry regiments were broken up and re-designated. So too were the armored regiments. Some of the tank elements remained in their divisions as tank battalions, others became separate non-divisional tank battalions, and others disbanded.

The 1943 re-organization did not mean, however, that the number of tanks in an armored division was halved, as had happened in the case of the British armored division in 1942 when one of the two armored brigades was removed. Within each new tank battalion there was an increase from three tank companies to four, and instead of there being light battalions and medium battalions there was now only a single type of tank battalion, three of its companies equipped with medium tanks, and one with light tanks. In addition each tank battalion had a headquarters company and a service company. The tank strength of the division was now 263—about one third less than under the "heavy" table.

Other changes in the "light" armored division included the addition of a third combat command which had the task of controlling the division's reserve on the march and hence was known as the reserve command, CCR, or sometimes as CCC. The armored reconnaissance battalion of the division was changed to a cavalry reconnaissance squadron, taking in the reconnaissance companies from the armored regiments as its troops. The divisional strength fell by almost 4,000 to 10,937.

As mentioned above, the 2nd and 3rd Armored Divisions remained as "heavy" divisions until the end of the war, each with two armored regiments (the 66th and 67th, and the 32nd and 33rd respectively), and one armored infantry regiment (the 41st and 36th respectively). The armored field artillery battalions of the 2nd Armored Division were the 14th, 78th, and 92nd, and of the 3rd Armored Division they were the 54th, 67th, and 391st. The 2nd's armored reconnaissance battalion was the 82nd, and the 3rd's was the 83rd.

After the 1943 re-organization had been applied to the other armored divisions (and it was not applied to the 1st Armored Division in Italy until July 20, 1944), their final normal make-up according to official sources was:

Armored Division	Tank Battalions	Armored Infantry Battalions	Armored Field Artillery Battalions	Cavalry Reconnaissance Squadron
1st	1st, 4th, 13th	6th, 11th, 14th	27th, 68th, 91st	81st
4th	8th, 35th, 37th	10th, 51st, 53rd	22nd, 66th, 94th	25th
5th	10th, 34th, 81st	15th, 46th, 47th	47th, 71st, 95th	85th
6th	15th, 68th, 69th	9th, 44th, 50th	69th, 128th, 212th, 231st	86th
7th	17th, 31st, 40th	23rd, 38th, 48th	434th, 440th, 489th	87th
8th	18th, 36th, 80th	7th, 49th, 58th	398th, 399th, 405th	88th
9th	2nd, 14th, 19th	27th, 52nd, 60th	3rd, 16th, 73rd	89th
10th	3rd, 11th, 21st	20th, 54th, 61st	419th, 420th, 423rd	90th
11th	22nd, 32nd, 41st	21st, 55th, 63rd	490th, 491st, 492nd	41st
12th	23rd, 43rd	17th, 56th, 66th	493rd, 494th, 495th	92nd
13th	24th, 45th	16th, 59th	496th, 497th, 498th	93rd
14th	25th, 47th, 48th	19th, 62nd, 68th	499th, 500th, 501st	94th
16th	5th, 16th, 26th	18th, 64th, 69th	395th, 396th, 397th	23rd
20th	9th, 20th, 27th	8th, 65th, 70th	413th	33rd

M4A1 Medium tanks (Shermans) on the assembly line at Lima Locomotive Works. M4A1 had a cast hull. The Sherman was produced in greater numbers than any other American tank.
(U.S. Army 140897)

It will be noticed that the 6th, 12th, 13th, and 20th Armored Divisions all varied from the norm in one way or another. The 6th had an extra artillery battalion, the 12th and 13th had only two tank battalions each, the 13th had only two infantry battalions, and the 20th had only one artillery battalion. As well as the units listed in the table each armored division also had an engineer battalion, a signals company, and supply, transport, and medical troops.

One armored infantry battalion (the 520th) and sixteen armored field artillery battalions (58th, 59th, 62nd, 65th, 93rd, 253rd, 274th, 275th, 276th, 342nd, 400th, 412th, 414th, 695th, 696th, and 1125th) are in the official list as well as those shown in the table. None are listed as organic units of any particular armored division. The 1125th served in Italy, all the others in the North-West Europe campaign.

THE ARMORED CORPS

When the 1st and 2nd Armored Divisions were organized in July 1940 they were put under command of the newly activated I Armored Corps. As the number of armored divisions increased so too did the armored corps. The II was organized in February 1942, the III on August 20, 1942, and the IV on September 5, 1942. This was in accordance with the doctrine then current—and not only in the American Army—that armored divisions should be employed in special corps. In the case of the U.S. Army the composition of an armored corps was two armored divisions and a motorized infantry division. By the end of 1943, however, the attitude to armored forces had changed somewhat from the mystical reverence with which they had been regarded after the panzer divisions' miraculous progress through Flanders and France in 1940. The growth of armored forces—and the same process can be seen at work in Germany and Britain as well as in the United States—had not been achieved without arousing the resentment of orthodox military opinion which disliked the aura of a "private army" that surrounded the armored formations. There were always those lurking in high places who were ready to cut armor down to size whenever the opportunity offered. The fact that by the end of 1943 armor had shown itself to be not always all-conquering under all circumstances allowed its critics to re-assert themselves powerfully. The "separateness" of the armored forces disappeared. The Armored Force itself became the Armored Command on July 2, 1943, and then merely the Armored Centre on February 20, 1944. By then, all armored units had been assigned to corps and armies and the doctrine of using mass armor was replaced by the doctrine of attrition through firepower. The armored corps were re-designated. The II, III, and IV Armored Corps became XVIII, XIX, and XX Corps respectively, while I Armored Corps was inactivated in North Africa and its staff used in the formation of Seventh Army headquarters.

SEPARATE (NON-DIVISIONAL) TANK BATTALIONS

The Armored Force started with the 1st and 2nd Armored Divisions and with one separate battalion that was not assigned to a division. This was the 70th Tank Battalion.

At the same time as the number of armored divisions was increasing rapidly so too were the number of separate tank battalions. The first four to join the 70th early in 1941 were the 191st, 192nd, 193rd, and 194th, which were organized from eighteen National Guard divisional tank companies. The 192nd and 194th, both light tank battalions, went straight to the Pacific where they were assigned to the Provisional Tank Group and fought in the first Philippine Islands campaign. The 193rd also went to the Pacific later, while the 191st fought first in Italy and then took part in the landings in the French Riviera in August 1944 and fought through to the end of the campaign in France and Germany.

Ten Regular Army separate tank battalions were constituted in 1941, as the 71st through the 80th Tank Battalions. These designations were soon changed to the 751st through the 760th. Most of the battalions fought in the Italian campaign. The 751st and 752nd fought in North Africa and Italy; the 753rd in Italy, then in the French Riviera landings, and in France and Germany; the 755th, 757th, 758th, and 760th in Italy; the 756th in North Africa, Italy, the French Riviera landings, France and Germany. The only two of the ten that did not take part in the Italian campaign were the 754th which was in the Pacific and the second Philippine Islands campaigns, and the 759th which was in Northern France and Germany.

The number of separate tank battalions continued to increase until by the end of 1944 a peak of 65 was reached, compared with 52 tank battalions that were part of armored divisions. In addition to these 65, there were another 29 in course of organization and there were 17 amphibian tractor battalions.

All but seven of the separate tank battalions (an exception which includes the 70th and the 191st through the 194th) were numbered in the 700 series. The other two exceptions were the 44th which fought in the Pacific and the second Philippines campaigns, and the 46th which took part in the North-West Europe campaign.

Some of the separate tank battalions after 1943 were spin-offs from the breaking up of the armored regiments in the armored divisions. These battalions were re-designated in the 700 series. In each armored division (except the 1st which produced no spin-off battalions, and, of course, the 2nd and 3rd which retained their armored regiments throughout the war) one of the armored regiments had one of its tank battalions re-designated consecutively from 706 onwards, while the other armored regiment had one of its tank battalions re-designated consecutively from 771 onwards. For example: from the 4th Armored Division the 35th Armored Regiment spun off the 771st Tank Battalion, and the 37th Armored Regiment spun off the 706th Tank Battalion; from the 5th Armored Division the 34th Armored Regiment spun off the 772nd Tank Battalion, and the 81st Armored Regiment spun off 707th Tank Battalion; from the 6th Armored Division the 68th Armored Regiment spun off the 773rd Tank Battalion, and the 69th Armored Regiment spun off the 708th Tank Battalion. The 774th and 709th Tank Battalions came from the 7th Armored Division, the 775th and 710th from the 8th, the 776th and 711th from the 9th, the 777th and 712th from the 10th—and so on. There were a few exceptions to this in that one or two of the later-formed armored divisions did not spin off two battalions.

A little over half the spun off tank battalions served in Europe (other than Italy), the remainder in the Pacific,

M5 Light tank under test during the development of wading devices. (U.S. Ordnance Department)

M5 Light tank under test at General Motors Proving Ground. (General Motors Corporation)

M3 Light tank with M1A1 Flamethrower mounted in place of the bow machine-gun under test in the Pacific theater. (U.S. Army)

M5A1 Light tank equipped for wading. (Courtesy G. B. Jarrett)

including in the case of five (the 706th, 710th, 716th, 775th, and 780th) the Philippines. The separate tank battalions serving in the different theaters were as follows:

Separate Tank Battalions and the Campaigns in which they fought

NOTE: Tank Battalions 1st through 5th, 8th through 11th, 13th through 27th, 31st and 32nd, 34th through 37th, 40th and 41st, 43rd, 45th, 47th and 48th, 68th and 69th, 80th and 81st, were all in armored divisions (see p. 21). Europe = the 1944–45 campaign.

44th	Pacific, Philippines
46th	Europe
70th	North Africa, Europe (D-Day DD tanks)*
191st	Italy, Southern France*, Europe
192nd	Philippines
193rd	Pacific
194th	Philippines
701st	Europe
702nd	Europe
706th	Pacific, Philippines
707th	Europe
708th (Amphibian)	Pacific
709th	Europe
710th	Pacific, Philippines
711th	Pacific
712th	Europe
713th (Flamethrower)	Pacific
714th	Europe
716th	Philippines
717th	Europe
735th	Europe
736th	Europe (DD tanks for Rhine crossing)*
737th	Europe
738th	Europe
739th	Europe
740th	Europe
741st	Europe (D-Day DD tanks)*
743rd	Europe (D-Day DD tanks)*
744th	Europe
745th	Europe
746th	Europe
747th	Europe
748th	Europe
749th	Europe
750th	Europe, Pacific
751st (originally 71st)	North Africa, Italy
752nd (originally 72nd)	North Africa, Italy
753rd (originally 73rd)	Italy, Southern France*, Europe
754th (originally 74th)	Pacific, Philippines
755th (originally 75th)	Italy
756th (originally 76th)	North Africa, Italy, Southern France*, Europe
757th (originally 77th)	Italy
758th (originally 78th)	Italy
759th (originally 79th)	Europe
760th (originally 80th)	Italy
761st	Europe
762nd	Pacific
763rd	Pacific, Philippines
766th	Pacific
767th	Pacific, Philippines
771st	Europe
772nd	Europe
773rd (Amphibian)	Pacific
774th	Europe
775th	Pacific, Philippines
776th (Amphibian)	Pacific, Philippines
777th	Europe
778th	Europe
780th (Amphibian)	Pacific, Philippines
781st	Europe
782nd	Europe
784th	Europe
786th	Europe
787th	Europe
798th (Amphibian)	Pacific

* Three tank battalions (the 70th, 741st, and 743rd) were trained in the operation of DD swimming tanks at B Wing of the British 79th Armoured Division on the Solent. They took part in the D-Day assault on the Normandy beaches on June 6, 1944. The 70th Tank Battalion was in support of 4th U.S. Infantry Division of VII Corps on Utah beach. It launched 30 tanks at 3,000 yards; one foundered. The 741st and 743rd Tank Battalions were in support of 1st U.S. Infantry Division of V Corps. The 741st launched 29 tanks at 6,000 yards; 27 foundered, 2 swam in. Three tanks were beached from LCTs. The 743rd did not launch any tanks, all were beached from LCTs. A company from the 736th Tank Battalion was given DD training at G Wing of the 79th Armoured Division on the River Maas north of Maastricht in March 1945 in preparation for the Rhine crossing at the end of the month. DD tanks were also included in the equipment of the tank battalions in Operation Anvil, the landings on the French Riviera in Southern France in August 1944, the 191st, the 753rd, and the 756th.

Two of the amphibian tank battalions (the 708th and 773rd) were re-organized as amphibian tractor battalions. There were also another 17 amphibian tractor battalions:

3rd (Provisional)	Pacific
4th	Pacific
80th	Europe
534th	Pacific
536th	Pacific, Philippines
539th	Philippines
540th	Philippines
658th	Pacific, Philippines
672nd	Pacific, Philippines
715th	Pacific
718th	Pacific, Philippines
726th	Pacific
727th	Pacific, Philippines
728th	Pacific, Philippines
733rd	Pacific
788th	Pacific, Philippines
826th	Pacific, Philippines

In addition to all the tank battalions and amphibian tractor battalions listed above there were four independent tank companies:

11th	Pacific
37th (Provisional Amphibian)	Philippines
602nd	Aleutians
603rd	Philippines

and one Anti-Aircraft Automotive Weapons Battalion, the 430th, which served in Europe.

The creation of the separate tank battalions was a recognition, even by armored division enthusiasts, that tanks would still be needed for close support of infantry. If non-divisional tank battalions were not organized to fill this need it seemed more than likely that it would be met by stripping the armored divisions of some of their tank battalions. To obviate this danger the separate tank battalions were formed specifically to work with infantry divisions, normally one battalion to a division. In due course, as we have seen, it turned out that the armored divisions were over-loaded with tank units and they stripped themselves, as it were, of a number of tank battalions which became separate battalions and were assigned to working with infantry divisions—the very situation they had been guarding against in the early days of the Armored Force!

Because of their infantry support mission the separate battalions were originally organized very similarly to the infantry tank battalions of the inter-war years. After the 1943 re-organization of the armored divisions had eliminated the two types of tank battalion, medium and light, in the division and substituted a single type with three medium companies and one light company, the separate tank battalions were also re-organized so that the non-divisional battalion became interchangeable with the tank battalion of an armored division. This simplified training, supply, reinforcement, and administration.

Just as there had been a Tank Group Headquarters for the five tank battalions in the 1920s, so the new separate tank battalions were put under the control of tank group headquarters, five battalions to each HQ. The 1st Tank Group was created on February 10, 1941 to supervise the first five tank battalions. The 2nd and 3rd Provisional Tank Groups were created on May 26, 1941. In February 1942 the number of battalions in a group was reduced to three.

The primary task of the tank group HQ was to supervise training, but it was sometimes also called upon

Shermans in the Italian campaign often functioned as artillery. As well as the 1st Armored Division eight separate non-divisional tank battalions fought in Italy. These are tanks of 755th Tank Battalion, October 1944. (U.S. Army SC195563)

Dug-in Sherman of 67th Armored Regiment 2nd Armored Division, on the German frontier in October 1944 using its firepower but not its mobility. (U.S. Army SC195335)

to undertake a combat mission. At least two groups were expanded by the inclusion of other arms and fought in Europe as sort of individual combat commands. One of these was the 1st Armored Group, activated at Fort Knox, Kentucky, on March 2, 1943, and re-designated on November 20, 1943 as 17th Armored Group. The other was the 11th Armoured Group. There were also the 13th and 20th Armored Groups which fought in the later Pacific campaigns. In general, however, "the tank group set-up was unworkable," writes Colonel Robert J. Icks. "The battalions never were sure who was in command since they received instructions not only from the Group but also from the Infantry, the Armored Force, and the Corps Area in which they happened to find themselves. In addition, the employment of tank groups in mass which had been anticipated originally never materialized and thus it not only was a useless tactical creation but it never commanded even administratively." Tank groups and separate battalions were assigned to armies or to GHQ for use as needed.

CAVALRY

As well as the 1st Armored Division, two others, the 9th and the 10th, formed their armored regiments from the cavalry. The question of what to do with the cavalry, according to the official Armor-Cavalry history, was "one of the most perplexing problems confronting the U.S. Army" as World War II approached and after the creation of the Armored Force. "During the years of peace when economy had been the keynote for U.S. military forces, it had been easy to shunt this problem aside; but now, with danger to the free world increasing and partial mobilization already under way, the Army had to face up to how to organize and equip its cavalry."*

According to the Armor-Cavalry history the National Defense Act of 1920 provided for two cavalry divisions, the 1st and the 2nd, of which the 1st was active and the 2nd inactive**. Each division had two cavalry brigades, each with two regiments, a machine-gun squadron, and a headquarters troop. There was also a horse artillery battalion with 75-mm. guns, a mounted engineer battalion, an ambulance company, the division trains, and the special troops (headquarters, signal, ordnance, and veterinary). A close analysis of the cavalry regiments' lineages, however, reveals that, on paper at least, there was also a 3rd Cavalry Division. The assignments of the cavalry regiments to the three divisions was as follows:

The 1st Cavalry Division started in 1921 with the 1st, 7th, 8th, and 10th Cavalry. In 1922 the 5th Cavalry replaced the 10th which was assigned to the 2nd Cavalry Division. In 1933 the 12th Cavalry replaced the 1st Cavalry which began its mechanization career. The final state of the division, therefore, as regards its horse regiments, was the 5th, 7th, 8th, and 12th Cavalry.

---

* Op. cit. p. 70.   ** p. 53.

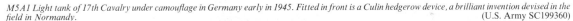

M5A1 Light tank of 17th Cavalry under camouflage in Germany early in 1945. Fitted in front is a Culin hedgerow device, a brilliant invention devised in the field in Normandy.
(U.S. Army SC199360)

The 2nd Cavalry Division started in 1923 with the 10th (ex-1st Cav. Div.) and the 12th Cavalry. In 1927 the 2nd Cavalry replaced the 10th which was assigned to the 3rd Cavalry Division. In 1933 the 11th and 13th Cavalry came into the division and the 12th was assigned to the 1st Cavalry Division in place of the 1st Cavalry. In 1936 the 13th Cavalry left the division to begin its mechanization career with 1st Cavalry in the 7th Cavalry Brigade (Mechanized), the predecessor of the 1st Armored Division. In 1940 the 9th Cavalry replaced the 11th and the 10th joined the division from the 3rd Cavalry Division. In 1941 the 14th Cavalry joined the division. Its final state therefore, as regards its horse regiments, was the 2nd, 9th, 10th and 14th Cavalry.

The 3rd Cavalry Division started in 1927 with the 6th and 10th Cavalry (ex-2nd Cav. Div.). In 1933 the 9th Cavalry was assigned to the division. In 1939 the 6th Cavalry ceased to be assigned to the division, and in 1940 the 9th and 10th Cavalry were reassigned to the 2nd Cavalry Division.

Cavalrymen, as we have seen earlier, were not of one mind about the military value of the horse. Some were in favor of pensioning it off and mechanizing the cavalry completely, others took a diametrically opposed view and wanted no mechanization at all, and others again favored a combination of horses and machines. One of the "combinationers" was the last Chief of Cavalry, Major General John K. Herr, who declared in 1938 that "we must not be misled to our own detriment to assume that the untried machine can displace the proved and tried horse," and the following year told a Congressional committee that "although in some cavalry missions it may be better to use horse cavalry alone or mechanized cavalry alone, on the whole the best results can be accomplished by using them together."

The "combination" organization was applied to two cavalry regiments, the 4th and the 6th, which by 1940

"Calliope" rocket projector, so named from its resemblance to a circus steam-pipe organ. It was mounted on a Sherman. (U.S. Ordnance Magazine)

Under the Combat Arms Regimental System (CARS) there are thirty-four parent regiments of armor and cavalry. Each has either a coat of arms or a historic badge. A complete coat of arms consists of a shield, a crest, and a motto. Historic badges are not shield-shaped but include mottoes.

1st Cavalry

2d Armored Cavalry

3d Armored Cavalry

4th Cavalry

5th Cavalry

6th Armored Cavalry

7th Cavalry

8th Cavalry

A "Calliope" T34 rocket launcher mounted on a Sherman fired rounds so rapidly that two successive rounds appeared to be fired simultaneously. Seen here is a "Calliope" of 134th Ordnance Battalion, 14th Armored Division, XXI Corps, Seventh Army, firing in the Fletrange area on the eastern frontier of France.
(U.S. Army Courtesy Col. G. B. Jarrett)

were partially horsed and partially mechanized. With two other regiments, the 1st and 13th, fully mechanized and in the 1st Armored Division, this left only the 3rd and 11th Cavalry as non-divisional mounted regiments.

In March 1942 the office of the Chief of Cavalry was eliminated with those of the other chiefs of arms when Army Ground Forces was formed. The pace of mechanization consequently quickened.

On July 15, 1942 the 9th and 10th Armored Divisions were activated, the 9th with the 2nd and 14th Armored Regiments, the 10th with the 3rd and 11th Armored Regiments. These four armored regiments were all constituted in the Army of the United States on July 11, 1942 and activated on the 15th with personnel and equipment from the 2nd, 3rd, 11th, and 14th Cavalry respectively which were all inactivated (although only temporarily, as it turned out) on that date. The 3rd Armored Regiment, it should be noted, is not to be confused with the original 3rd Armored Regiment in 3rd Armored Division which was re-designated the 33rd Armored Regiment on May 8, 1941.

The inactivation of the 2nd and 14th Cavalry still left the 2nd Cavalry Division with one of its two cavalry brigades, the 4th, which had the 9th and 10th Cavalry; this brigade remained active. The 1st Cavalry Division also remained active. Both divisions went overseas, though neither took horses with them. The 1st Cavalry Division fought in four major campaigns in the South-West Pacific as a light infantry division. It retained the

four-regiment, two-brigade formation of the cavalry division, but had 4,000 fewer men than the standard infantry division of 15,000 men. It also lacked the standard 155-mm. howitzer field artillery battalion, but special allowances of heavy weapons and other infantry-type equipment were supplied to compensate for this. The 2nd Cavalry Division was fully reactivated in February 1943 and served in North Africa, though it did not fight as a unit. Its existence, however, was short-lived. Between February and May 1944 it was completely inactivated and its personnel were transferred to service units.

While the cavalry regiments in the 1st and 2nd Cavalry Divisions were being dismounted, even if not mechanized, the remainder of the regiments—and these included the 15th, 16th, and 17th Cavalry which were reactivated, and seven partially horsed-partially mechanized National Guard cavalry regiments in Federal service*—were now mechanized completely. Further-

---

* These were the 101st (New York), 102nd (New Jersey), 104th (Pennsylvania), 106th (Illinois), 107th (Ohio), 113th (Iowa), and the 115th (Wyoming). A National Guard brigade of two horse regiments (the 112th and 124th Cavalry (Texas)) also entered Federal service. The two regiments were dismounted, withdrawn from the brigade, and reorganized as infantry; the HQ and HQ troop of the brigade (the 56th Cavalry) became the 56th Reconnaissance Troop, Mechanized.

more the 2nd, 3rd, 11th, and 14th Cavalry were re-activated as mechanized cavalry units, the armored regiments that had stemmed from them becoming newly constituted units instead of re-designated ones. In 1943 and 1944 these non-divisional mechanized cavalry regiments were broken up to form separate mechanized cavalry groups and squadrons, for by now the problem of what to do with the cavalry had been solved: horses were banished and the job of mechanized cavalry was reconnaissance.**

Each mechanized cavalry group consisted of HQ, HQ troop, and two or more attached mechanized cavalry reconnaissance squadrons. Groups were assigned to armies and then allotted to corps within the army. Frequently a group was attached to a division—usually an infantry division—for operations. Despite the directive issued by the War Department in 1943 that mechanized cavalry units were "to engage in combat only to the extent necessary to accomplish their missions" of reconnaissance, the practice of the battlefield turned out

---

** Although the last horse cavalry unit to fight mounted was the 26th Cavalry of the Philippine Scouts early in 1942, there were instances of provisionally organized units using horses in the U.S. Army after that. "Merrill's Marauders" had horses in the Indo-Burmese theater. So too had the 3rd Infantry Division's Reconnaissance Troop in Sicily and the early part of the Italian campaign.

somewhat different from the theory of the War Department's directive. A fascinating analysis in the official Armor-Cavalry history (p. 73) shows that purely reconnaissance missions for mechanized cavalry in Europe—where most of the mechanized cavalry units fought— were extremely rare. Indeed they accounted for only three per cent of the missions assigned. Most frequent were defensive missions (33 per cent), followed by special operations, "including acting as mobile reserve, providing for security and control of rear areas, and operating as an army information service" (29 per cent), security missions i.e. "blocking, screening, protecting flanks, maintaining contact between larger units, and filling gaps" (25 per cent), and offensive missions (10 per cent). "For offensive, defensive, and security missions, the mechanized cavalry group was normally reinforced by a battalion of field artillery, a battalion of tank destroyers, and a company of combat engineers."

As well as the 73 non-divisional mechanized cavalry units that were active in World War II as groups and squadrons, there were also well over 100 divisional cavalry units—indeed there were virtually as many as there were divisions in the Army. Each infantry division had its cavalry reconnaissance troop, designated by the same number as the division of which it was a part e.g. 1st Cavalry Reconnaissance Troop was in 1st Infantry Division and fought with it in Italy and in the North-

One of the very rare vehicles in the U.S. Army in World War II was the M4A1E8 seen here in combat in Europe. It was the early 1944 prototype for the production M4A1 (76-mm) with wet stowage and HVSS. (U.S. Army)

9th Cavalry

10th Cavalry

11th Armored Cavalry

12th Cavalry

13th Cavalry

14th Armored Cavalry

15th Cavalry

16th Armor

17th Cavalry

32d Armor

33d Armor

34th Armor

35th Armor

37th Armor

40th Armor

63d Armor

64th Armor

66th Armor

M10 Tank Destroyer of 36th Infantry Division passing a knocked out Sherman in the fighting for Oberhoffen, eastern France, March 1945. In the background a casualty is being removed by medics. (U.S. Army 199935)

Mines are the tank's enemy: a desolate Sherman after hitting a mine in the European Theater on November 21, 1944.   (U.S. Army)

West Europe campaign from the beaches of Normandy onwards. The 1st Cavalry Division (which, it will be remembered, fought in the Pacific as a light infantry division) had the 302nd Cavalry Reconnaissance Troop —the 301st, incidentally, was a troop that served in the Aleutians. Each armored division also had its divisional cavalry unit. As mentioned earlier the 1st Armored Divisions was originally constituted in the Regular Army on April 22, 1940 and activated at Fort Knox on June 1, as 7th Reconnaissance and Support Squadron (Mechanized)—its numerical designation coming, no doubt, from the 7th Cavalry Brigade (Mechanized)—and was re-organized and re-designated on July 15, 1940 (the day the division was activated and on which the unit was assigned to it) as the 1st Reconnaissance Battalion (Armored). The unit was re-designated three times during World War II: first, on May 8, 1941, as 81st Reconnaissance Battalion (Armored); second, on January 1, 1942, as 81st Armored Reconnaissance Battalion; and third, on July 20, 1944, when the division changed from a "heavy" to a "light" armored division, as 81st Cavalry Reconnaissance Squadron, Mechanized.

The designation "armored reconnaissance battalion" was applied to the mechanized cavalry unit of the heavy armored division, and the designation "cavalry reconnaissance squadron, mechanized" to the mechanized cavalry unit of the light armored division. The 2nd and 3rd Armored Divisions which remained under the "heavy" table had the 82nd and 83rd Armored Reconnaissanc‹ · Battalions respectively,* while the final desig-

* Their original designations were respectively, 2nd Reconnaissance Battalion (Armored) constituted on July 15, 1940, and 3rd Reconnaissance Battalion (Armored) constituted on January 16, 1941.

nations of the cavalry reconnaissance squadrons in the other armored divisions are given in an earlier Table (p. 21). The other cavalry reconnaissance squadrons, all of which served in the European theater were:
2nd, 3rd, 4th, 6th, 15th, 16th, 17th, 18th, 19th, 24th, 28th, 32nd, 36th, 38th, 42nd, 43rd, 44th, 91st, 101st, 102nd, 104th, 106th, 107th, 113th, 116th, 117th, 121st, 125th. (The lineage of those from 2nd through 17th, 19th, 24th, 28th, 42nd, and 43rd, as well as the majority of the armored divisions' cavalry reconnaissance squadrons stemmed from the cavalry regiments).

TANK DESTROYERS

A perennial argument in armored circles was whether the best anti-tank weapon was a gun or another tank. Although the latter doctrine had many supporters among American military leaders it was the former that prevailed. For the destruction of enemy armor the U.S. Army had tank destroyer battalions, equipped with self-propelled or towed high velocity guns.

The tank destroyer battalions had their tactical origin in the 1940 maneuvers and in the traumatic effect of the German *blitzkrieg*. "The German successes," says the official Armor-Cavalry history, "were adversely affecting morale of combat troops, and there was an urgent need for new, effective weapons to calm their fears and prove the vulnerability of the tank."* The War Department decided that tanks should be countered by fast-moving, high velocity guns used en masse.

* Op. cit. p. 67.

35

67th Armor

68th Armor

69th Armor

70th Armor

72d Armor

73d Armor

77th Armor

81st Armor

© Profile Publications Ltd.

M10 Tank Destroyers of 601st Tank Destroyer Battalion, 45th Infantry Division, cross the Durance River in Provence during Operation Anvil—the Allied landings in the south of France, August 1944. Although planned and generally known as Anvil the Operation was actually carried out as Dragoon.
(U.S. Army)

Few anti-tank guns should be placed in static defensive positions; the majority should be held in mobile reserve, whence they should "seek, strike, and destroy" the main enemy armored thrusts.

At this period the infantry division's artillery regiment included a number of 37-mm. anti-tank guns. From the fall of 1940 each infantry regiment, of which there were three in the infantry division, had an anti-tank company added to it. This 14th Company in the regiment (there being three infantry battalions each with four companies and a 13th Company equipped with six 105-mm. howitzers) remained in the infantry regiment throughout the war, equipped at first with towed 37-mm. guns and later with six 57-mm. guns. The anti-tank units in the divisional artillery, however, were absorbed into the new anti-tank battalions which were organized in 1941 as a result of the War Department's doctrine of mass employment of mobile anti-tank guns. To impart an offensive spirit to these new units and to give them a psychological boost which would "prove the vulnerability of the tank" by stating the fact, their designation was changed in late 1941 to tank destroyer battalions.

The Tank Destroyer Center was set up at Fort Meade, Maryland, and then moved in February 1942 to the new Camp Hood, Texas. Although the Tank Destroyer force had no real standing as a separate arm it successfully resisted all attempts throughout the war to absorb it in the Armored Force or in any of the older arms. It grew prodigiously. By late 1942 it had 100,000 men and 80 active battalions, with 64 more planned. By early 1943 it reached its maximum with 106 active battalions—almost as many as the total number of tank battalions. Thereafter a decline set in, partly because the American troops in action had not had to face the massed armored formations that 1940 had seemed to make likely, and partly because tank destroyer units were used as reinforcements to replace the heavy casualties suffered by divisions in combat. By early 1944 the number of active battalions was 78, and there was a further decrease during the year.

The tank destroyer battalions serving in the different theaters were as follows:

85th	Europe (= the 1944–45 campaign)
601st	North Africa, Italy, Southern France, Europe
603rd	Europe
605th	Europe
607th	Europe
609th	Europe
610th	Europe
612th	Europe
614th	Europe
628th	Europe
629th	Europe
630th	Europe
631st	Europe
632nd	Pacific, Philippines
633rd	Europe
634th	Europe
635th	Europe
636th	Italy, Southern France, Europe
637th	Philippines
638th	Europe
640th	Pacific, Philippines
641st	Pacific
643rd	Europe
644th	Europe
645th	Italy, Southern France, Europe
648th	Europe
654th	Europe
656th	Europe
661st	Europe
679th	Italy
691st	Europe
692nd	Europe
701st	North Africa, Italy
702nd	Europe
703rd	Europe
704th	Europe
705th	Europe
738th	Europe
771st	Europe
772nd	Europe
773rd	Europe
774th	Europe
776th	Europe
786th	Europe
801st	Europe
802nd	Europe
803rd	Italy
804th	Europe
805th	North Africa, Italy
806th	Europe
807th	Europe
808th	Europe
809th	Europe
811th	Europe

M10A1 Self-Propelled Gun in combat in France in 1944. Both the M10 and the M10A1 had a 3-inch gun. The former was built on an adapted M4A2 chassis, the latter on an M4A3 chassis.

813th	North Africa, Italy, Southern France, Europe
814th	Europe
815th	Pacific
817th	Europe
818th	Europe
819th	Pacific
820th	Europe
822nd	Europe
823rd	Europe
824th	Europe
825th	Europe
827th	Europe
843rd	Europe
893rd	Europe
894th	North Africa, Italy
899th	North Africa, Europe

The original intention being that the tank destroyer battalions should be used in mass, formation head-quarters were set up to control them. Two brigades, the 1st and 2nd Tank Destroyer Brigades, were organized, and thirteen tank destroyer groups: the 1st through the 9th, the 12th, the 16th, the 20th, and the 23rd. All these saw action, except the 2nd T.D. Brigade which was inactivated in early 1944. However they did not see action as complete formations because the employment of tank destroyer battalions did not turn out as en-visaged in the early days. Instead they were used as assault guns and conventional motorized artillery even more frequently than in their rôle of direct tank des-troyers. The theory that tanks would not fight tanks was exploded on the battlefield and with it went the theory of the tank destroyers' exclusive rôle. The battalions were assigned to armies for re-assignment to divisions as needed.

The tank destroyer battalion had about 800 men and a total of 36 guns, together with strong reconnaissance and anti-aircraft elements. Approximately half the battalions were equipped with self-propelled guns, the other half with towed guns. Self-propelled tank destroyers were the M10 (and M10A1) with a 3-inch gun, the M18

(Hellcat) with a 76-mm. gun, and the M36 with a 90-mm. gun.

Despite the fine combat record of the Tank Destroyer force, battlefield experience showed that the lightly armored tank destroyer with its open top turret was a less effective anti-tank weapon than a better armed and armored tank. By the end of the war this proved to be unarguable and the Tank Destroyer force went out of existence.

U.S. MARINE CORPS ARMOR

In the early 1920s the U.S. Marine Corps had a few light tank companies equipped with the 6-ton tank which had been copied from the French Renault F.T. tank. Some experimenting was done with armored cars and with Marmon-Herrington light tanks, but the need for an amphibian tank was never met. A Christie amphibian tank was deck-loaded on a submarine and launched in a simulated landing assault on Culebra Island, east of Puerto Rico, in 1924, but it was not found suitable and no further development took place until the Roebling amphibian tractor was discovered by the Marine Corps in 1937. Three of these Alligators, as they were called, were purchased and tested, and in late 1940 funds were authorized to order 200. The first was delivered in July 1941. It was designated LVT 1 (Landing Vehicle Tracked). A series of LVTs was developed and used extensively in the Pacific campaigns in World War II. These Amtracs, as LVTs were also called, were employed both logistically and tactically, not only by the Marine Corps but also by the U.S. Army and by the British, Free French and Nationalist Chinese, to whom some were supplied.

After 1939 threats of American involvement in the European War led to more widespread amphibious training by the Marine Corps. Culebra Island was no longer suitable because of German U-boat operations in the Caribbean, so a new amphibious training base was established in North Carolina.

Organizational changes were made at the same time. The 1st Marine Division was organized out of three three-battalion infantry regiments, a four-battalion artillery regiment, a shore party engineer battalion, an engineer battalion, and other elements including a light tank battalion. This organization was soon altered to three infantry regiments, an artillery regiment with three pack howitzer battalions and one 105-mm. howitzer battalion, an engineer battalion, a light tank battalion, a special weapons battalion, a scout company, a signal company, an amphibian tractor battalion, a medical battalion, a service battalion, a guard company, and the divisional headquarters company. Then a second division was organized. Eventually six divisions plus separate regimental combat teams, auxiliary organizations, paratroops and air units were formed.

Sherman tanks were introduced with the landing at Tarawa in the South Pacific in November 1943, but without previous practice with infantry such as the light tanks had developed. Only one company of Shermans was available and most of them were casualties in this first operation. The growing inadequacy of the light tank led to the conversion of many to flamethrower tanks. Gradually Shermans replaced all light tanks in the divisional tank battalion.

In subsequent operations infantry regiments were assigned one reinforced medium tank company of 18 tanks plus a platoon of four flamethrower tanks and two light tanks. Unfortunately, lack of shipping often made it necessary to leave behind one out of the three medium tank companies in a divisional tank battalion. Operationally, it might have been better to have provided space for these tanks and to have reduced the number of infantry carried for a given operation, at least for the initial landing.

By the time of the landing on Iwo Jima in February 1945 the light flamethrower tanks had been replaced by flamethrowing Shermans. In fact most of the Shermans had flamethrowing capability, but of these the most effective, because of their longer range, were those which

Loading a Christie amphibious tank on to a submarine for U.S. Marine Corps maneuvers off Puerto Rico in 1924. This proved to be a blind alley; the LVT or Amtrac became the Marine Corps assault vehicle. (Defense Department (Marine Corps) 528927)

Successive waves of LVT 3s forming and moving shoreward at Iwo Jima.

(Photo: U.S. Navy 50-G 312456)

An LVT 2 with bolt-on armor pulling a disabled LVT 4 on Leyte Island.
(Photo: U.S. Army No. SC 260617)

fired through the 75-mm. gun tube rather than from the machine-gun port in the front plate.

In the operation on Okinawa in April 1945 the Japanese developed an efficient defensive system against the tank-infantry teams. They first sought to eliminate the infantry by high volume fire and then turned high volume fire on to the tank. If this failed, anti-tank assault teams with satchel charges would try, under cover of smoke, to destroy the tank. Nevertheless, the American use of tanks on Okinawa reached a high peak as evidenced by a dispatch issued by General Ushijima shortly before his death and found later: "The enemy's power lies in his tanks. It has become obvious that our general battle against the American Forces is a battle against their . . . tanks."*

Often on Okinawa, two relays of tanks were used in order to permit rearming so as to maintain a continuous attack on caves and bunkers. This technique of the tank-infantry team was called by the U.S. commander the "blowtorch and corkscrew" method, the former being the Shermans with flamethrowers, and the latter being demolition devices.

* Quoted from report of CG 1st Marine Division in The U.S. Marines and Amphibious War, by Peter A. Isely and Philip A. Crowl, Princeton University Press, Princeton, N.J., 1951.

Marines coming ashore in and debarking from their LVT 2 at Namur in the Kwajalein Atoll, February 1944. (Photo: courtesy U.S. Marine Corps)

Beach installations at Iwo Jima and Amtrac casualties four days later already partially buried in the soft volcanic ash. (Photo: U.S. Coast Guard)

Satan flamethrower M5 Light tanks of 13th Armored Group which fought in the Luzon, Philippines, campaign that began in January 1945.
(U.S. Army 417651)

IV
(1945–1950)

With the end of the war in Europe in May 1945 and in the Pacific three months later the Western Allies proceeded to demobilize rapidly. In the wholesale thinning down of American forces the formidable strength of the armored formations was destroyed, a weakness that was soon to cause concern when it became apparent that the U.S.S.R. was demobilizing much more slowly and was maintaining strong occupation forces in Eastern Europe.

Before the end of 1945 twelve of the sixteen armored divisions had been inactivated, leaving only the 1st, 2nd, 4th, and 20th. In March and April 1946 three more were inactivated, leaving only the 2nd.* The separate non-divisional tank battalions were inactivated with equal speed. For example, the four infantry divisions** on occupation duty in Japan each had a tank battalion

---

* For details of the divisions' inactivation see p. 54

** Including the 1st Cavalry Division which was organized as infantry. The other three divisions were the 7th, 24th, and 25th.

assigned to it, but only one company of each battalion was in fact organized and these companies were equipped with nothing more powerful than M24 Chaffee light tanks in case heavier tanks should damage Japanese roads and bridges. Even the Armored Center at Fort Knox was inactivated at the end of October 1945 and most of its functions were taken over by the Armored School.

There was, however, still an obvious prime need for mechanized if not for armored units in the U.S. occupation forces in Europe. These units had to be flexible in organization and highly mobile to carry out security duties, and they had to require the minimum of personnel, for men were in short supply in a rapidly demobilizing army that was getting back to a peace-time strength. Armor and cavalry units were chosen as being more adaptable for the task than other arms. They were re-organized and re-designated as elements of the U.S. Constabulary in Europe which became operational on July 1, 1946.

THE U.S. CONSTABULARY

The Constabulary consisted of the 1st, 2nd, and 3rd Constabulary Brigades, together with a Headquarters and a Headquarters Company. There were ten Constabulary Regiments assigned to the brigades—the 1st, 2nd, 3rd, 4th, 5th, 6th, 10th, 11th, 14th, and 15th. Regiments had an HQ and an HQ troop, two or three squadrons, a light tank troop, a motor-cycle platoon with 25 motor-cycles, and a horse platoon with 30 horses—so horses had not yet been banished from the Army after all!

Constabulary units were formed from elements of the 1st and 4th Armored Divisions, from cavalry groups and their constituent cavalry reconnaissance squadrons, and from a few separate tank battalions. All the tank battalions and the cavalry reconnaissance squadron of both the 1st and 4th Armored Divisions became Constabulary squadrons. The 1st Constabulary Regiment was formed basically from the 11th Armored Group, the 2nd Constabulary Regiment from the 2nd Cavalry Group, the 3rd from elements of the 1st and 4th Armored Divisions, the 4th from the 4th Cavalry Group and elements of the 6th Cavalry Group, the 5th from elements of the 4th Armored Division, the 6th from elements of the 6th Cavalry Group, the 10th from elements of the 1st Armored Division and from the 771st Tank Battalion, the 11th from the 11th Cavalry Group and elements of the 4th Armored Division, the 14th from the 14th Cavalry Group, and the 15th from the 15th Cavalry Group and elements of the 1st Armored Division.

The Constabulary, whose strength reached nearly 35,000 by early 1947, was by its very nature a transient

A T1E3 Mine Exploder mounted on a Sherman bogged down on the frontier of Germany, the week before Christmas 1944. A drawback of the "Aunt Jemima", as it was called, was that with each disc weighing three tons it sank like a stone into the mud of battle-mired roads. (U.S. Army)

organization that became outdated by the changing political situation and the confrontation between East and West in Europe. The HQ and HQ Company was inactivated in November 1950, and the U.S. Constabulary was superseded by the newly activated Seventh Army. However, the 2nd Constabulary Brigade and the 15th and 24th Constabulary Squadrons, from the 15th and 4th Constabulary Regiments respectively, continued to function until December 1952 when they were inactivated—the last of the Constabulary units.

Armored Force peeps and jeeps at the Siegfried Line—the West Wall of Germany. (Courtesy Col. G. B. Jarrett)

The dragon's teeth of the German West Wall were not as invulnerable as had been feared by the Allies. They were broken down by tank gunfire to create paths.

(U.S. Army)

The problem of assaulting the Siegfried Line loomed large—before the event. The M4A3E2 ("Jumbo") specially armored Sherman assault tank was built to breach these anti-tank defenses which propaganda had declared to be "impregnable". In point of fact artillery and tank fire created cavities in the dragon's teeth without undue trouble.

(U.S. Army)

ARMOR, CAVALRY, AND ARMORED CAVALRY

Fundamental to the future of armored forces in the U.S. Army was the need to get statutory authority for their existence as a separate arm of the service, and with that authority must go a decision as to what the arm should be called. The Armored Force had been created on July 10, 1940 "for purposes of service test" because there was no authorization for a separate armored branch. There was still no Congressional authorization after the war, despite the fact that armor enthusiasts regarded the tank as the main weapon of land warfare. Officers serving with armored units in the war had retained their basic branch. In 1947 armored officers began to be assigned to the cavalry branch and the War Department announced that it expected there would eventually be statutory approval of an armored cavalry arm to replace the cavalry. The marks of the old antagonism between tankmen and horsed cavalrymen—an antagonism which was equally strong in the British Army—revealed themselves in the proviso that, until that approval was given, tank officers would be detailed to the cavalry "unless they objected", and, by the same token, cavalry officers who did not desire to serve with armor could be "transferred to or detailed to other arms and services."

The term "armored cavalry" for the new arm pleased few of those involved. Those who had never served with horses thought that "armor" best described what it was all about. Others argued that the arm was still carrying out the functions of cavalry—mobility, firepower, and shock action—whatever it was mounted on; "cavalry" it should continue to be called. When statutory approval was finally given for the new arm in the Army Organization Act of 1950, it was given the name of "armor". It would be "a continuation of the cavalry."

Sandbags were among the "field fixes" to afford protection (mainly psychological in this case) against the devastating hand-held Panzerfaust. *This Sherman is leaving concealment in Niederbetschdorf on its way to the Rittershofen front on the eastern frontier of France, January 1945.*
(Courtesy Col. G. B. Jarrett)

Despite this decision and the unpopularity of the term "armored cavalry" it did not disappear from the U.S. Army. Five regiments perpetuated it in their designation as "armored cavalry regiments", and still do so. The first of these five regiments to be organized in this rôle was the 3rd Armored Cavalry, which, as 3rd Cavalry, had first been inactivated in 1942 to form 3rd Armored Regiment in 10th Armored Division and had then been re-activated and had formed 3rd Cavalry Group. It became an armored cavalry regiment in 1948. Later in the same year the 2nd, 6th, 11th, and 14th Armored Cavalry were organized from units of the U.S. Constabulary. All were activated except the 11th which was not activated until 1951 during the Korean War.

76-mm gun Sherman of 3rd Armored Division knocked out by German artillery fire at Bergerhausen near Cologne on January 3, 1945. Fifteen U.S. armored divisions served in the North-West Europe campaign—and another one in Italy.
(U.S. Army SC 201343–S)

Shermans and crews of 44th Battalion which led the drive into Manila, capital of the Philippines, in February 1945.

(U.S. Army 417650)

46

Logs were one of the "field fixes" applied to protect Shermans against German Panzerfaust *fire.*

(Courtesy Col J. B. Jarrett [U.S. Army SC197062])

At Grand Halleux, Belgium, tanks and jeeps of 75th Infantry Division are painted white to camouflage them from enemy ground and air observation in the bitter winter conditions that prevailed on the Western Front.
(ETOHQ 45–8805)

Shermans of 714th Battalion at Bischwiller, France, January 8, 1945, preparing to fire into Drusenheim. The 714th Battalion was a "spin-off" battalion from 12th Armored Division after September 1943. The 12th Armored Division, it will be noticed in the relevant table compiled from the official list, had only two, instead of three, organic tank battalions—the 23rd and 43rd. The official caption to this picture, however, suggests that the 12th Armored Division did in fact have a third tank battalion under command: the 714th, which was its own offspring. (U.S. Army SC198784)

The armored cavalry regiment of this period had three reconnaissance battalions as its main strength and was equipped with 72 light tanks and 69 medium tanks. Its primary rôle was described as being "to engage in security, light combat, and reconnaissance missions. The regiment is not designed to engage in combat with hostile armor or strongly organized defenses."

Since their inception the organization of the armored cavalry regiments has changed somewhat, the main difference being that each has an air cavalry troop and has added helicopters to its equipment. The traditional cavalry designations of squadrons and troops have replaced the battalion and company designations.

V
(SINCE 1950)

When the North Koreans attacked the South in June 1950 the only tanks near enough to be rushed into action were the M24 Chaffees of the four tank companies assigned to the occupation divisions in Japan. The companies were formed into a provisional tank battalion which first went into combat in support of the 24th Division on July 11. The enemy was equipped with T-34/85s. For over three weeks the light tanks had no support from heavier armor. Then in the first week of August five tank battalions arrived from the United States (the 6th, 70th, 72nd, 73rd, and 89th) equipped with medium tanks (Sherman "Easy Eights"—M4A3E8, M26 Pershings, and M46 Pattons) and the balance of armor was redressed. At the end of the month the British Commonwealth Division began to arrive, bringing with it Centurions. In early November the 64th Tank Battalion came to Korea with the 3rd Infantry Division.

The Korean War forced re-mobilization on the United States. As far as armor was concerned it brought eight National Guard infantry divisions into Federal service, each division with its organic tank battalion and

reconnaissance company, it brought the activation of a fifth armored cavalry regiment, and it saw the re-activation of four armored divisions, as well as the activation of tank battalions for the Regular Army infantry divisions.

The National Guard infantry divisions brought into Federal service were the 40th (California) and 45th (Oklahoma), both of which fought in Korea, the 28th (Pennsylvania) and 43rd (Connecticut, Rhode Island, and Vermont), both of which went to Germany, and the 31st (Alabama and Mississippi), 37th (Ohio), 44th (Illinois), and 47th (Minnesota and North Dakota), all of which became training centers for reinforcements.

None of the armored divisions or the five armored cavalry regiments served in Korea.

THE ARMORED DIVISIONS

At the outbreak of the Korean War only the 2nd and 3rd Armored Divisions were active. The 2nd had had an uninterrupted record of service since its activation on July 15, 1940; the 3rd had been inactivated in Germany on November 9, 1945 and then reactivated on July 17, 1947 as a training division. A third armored division, the 5th, had only recently been inactivated for the second time. Its first inactivation was on October 11, 1945; it had then been reactivated on July 6, 1948, only to be inactivated again on February 1, 1950. Soon after the beginning of the fighting in Korea, the 5th was reactivated yet again (on September 1, 1950), the first of the four armored divisions that were reactivated because of the Korean War.

The second of the armored divisions to be reactivated was the 6th (September 5, 1950), the third was the 7th (November 24, 1950), and the fourth was the 1st (March 7, 1951). Of the six armored divisions active in the Korean War only the 1st and 2nd were fully organized as combat divisions. The others were mainly training divisions. Only the 2nd went overseas—to Germany, in 1951.

After the Korean Armistice Agreement of July 27, 1953, the 7th Armored Division was soon inactivated (November 15, 1953), but the number of active armored

A winter-camouflaged Sherman of Company A, 701st Battalion, 9th U.S. Army, carrying both authorized and unauthorized stowage at Brachelen, Germany, January 1945. (U.S. Army Courtesy Col. G. B. Jarrett)

M36 Self-Propelled Gun of 3rd U.S. Army in Luxembourg, January 3, 1945. The M36, which had a 90-mm gun on the M10 chassis, could take on any German tank. (U.S. Army SC148613)

The Battle of the Bulge. A Sherman of 774th Battalion, 3rd U.S. Army, passes a knocked out German Panther in the forest near Bovigny, Belgium, January 17, 1945.

divisions was restored to six on June 15, 1954, when the 4th was reactivated. On March 15, 1955, the 3rd became a combat division. A year later, on March 16, 1956, the number of active armored divisions was reduced to four with the inactivation on that date of the 5th and 6th Armored Divisions. From 1957 to 1962 the 1st Armored Division was reduced to a single combat command. Thereafter it reverted to full organization.

The organization of an armored division was no longer what it had been in World War II. Towards the end of the war the need for more armored infantry in the division had been generally recognized and the War Department had under consideration a proposed structure which would increase the total divisional strength by 4,000 to about 15,000. The actual increase,

introduced in 1948, was to 15,973. The reserve command was augmented to allow it to function as a third combat command when required. A fourth infantry battalion was added and the number of companies in each battalion was increased from three to four, making 16 infantry companies in the division instead of the previous nine. The division was also given a battalion of heavy artillery (155-mm. self-propelled howitzers) and a battalion of self-propelled anti-aircraft guns to add to the three 105-mm. self-propelled howitzer battalions. The number of tank battalions was increased to four by the addition of a heavy tank battalion which was equipped with M103s. The reconnaissance battalion was retained. The total number of tanks in the division was 373. The first armored division to which this reorganization was

The Light Tank T7 with a mock-up of the Light Tank T7E2 on its right. The T7 became an attempt to replace the M4 Medium (Sherman), but it fell disastrously between the stools of light tank or medium tank. It was probably the best light tank of World War II—but at its fruition nobody wanted a light tank. A sad end to a good tank.
(U.S. Ordnance Department)

applied was the 2nd which ceased to be a wartime "heavy" division when its armored regiments were broken up in March 1946.

Two further reorganizations have taken place since the Korean War, both made necessary by "developments in nuclear weapons that made wide dispersion, high mobility, and great flexibility—without loss of massed firepower—mandatory characteristics for military forces. Combat areas of future nuclear wars were viewed as much broader and deeper than battlefields of the past, requiring small, self-contained, fast-moving units. Speed was imperative not only in the concentration of forces for attack but also in dispersion for defense. On the other hand, the Army had to retain its ability to fight limited or non-nuclear wars, where the requirements for mobility or dispersion were not as important."*

The first reorganization was the pentomic (or pentana) plan which had been applied to all armored divisions by mid-1958. Little change was needed in the basic structure because the combat command set-up already provided the essential flexibility. As far as the tanks were concerned there were still four battalions, but all four were now similarly equipped—the heavy M103s with their 120-mm. guns were withdrawn from Army service. The total number of tanks was 360—306 of them with 90-mm. guns, and 54 with 76-mm. guns. The number of armored infantry and field artillery battalions remained the same, but—and it was here that the greatest change took place—the artillery was given an atomic capability. The division's strength was 14,617.

_____

* Official Armor-Cavalry history, op. cit. p. 80.

The second reorganization of divisions known as ROAD (Reorganization Objective Army Divisions) was completed in 1964. This gave the Army four types of division—airborne, infantry, armored, and mechanized. All four had a fundamental similarity with their own reconnaissance, artillery, and support units, and with three brigade headquarters, corresponding in the case of the armored division to its old combat commands. The difference between the divisions occurred in the number of tank and infantry battalions which varied according to the mission and other relevant factors. The change in the armored division, because of the continuance of combat commands albeit under the title of brigade headquarters, was less than in the other types of division.

A ROAD armored division had a divisional base with four artillery battalions, an engineer battalion and other support units, and an armored cavalry squadron of 18 light tanks. As its maneuver elements it had six tank battalions and five mechanized infantry battalions. And it had three brigade headquarters to which the various units could be assigned. Each tank battalion had 54 medium and two light tanks, and each mechanized infantry battalion had two light tanks. This gave the division a total of 40 light tanks (including the armored cavalry's), and 324 medium or main battle tanks. Its total strength was 15,966.

The armored cavalry squadron in all four types of division had an air cavalry troop equipped with helicopters.

In 1965 the 1st Cavalry Division was reorganized as a fifth type of division—airmobile—and was sent to fight in Vietnam.

The Light Tank T7E2 was a splendid vehicle which user demands converted to the totally inadequate Medium Tank M7.   (U.S. Ordnance Department)

The Medium Tank M7 was intended as a replacement for the M4 Sherman, but was incapable of becoming so because its weight had been so enhanced that it was badly underpowered. Production continued to be concentrated on the more efficient vehicle—the M4 Sherman. (John Kennon)

M22 Airborne Light Tank training with infantry at Fort Knox. In fact none was used by U.S. troops in combat, and only a few by the British who called the tank the Locust. (Courtesy Marmom-Herrington Co.)

M24 Light tank, called the Chaffee by the British, saw only limited service in World War II but bore the brunt of the initial North Korean attack in July 1950. This M24 Chaffee is fitted with 23-inch experimental offset grouser track for improving flotation. (U.S. Ordnance Department)

The bridge over the River Rhine; the bridge at Remagen which was captured intact by 9th Armored Division on March 7, 1945.

(U.S. Army)

The final status of the armored divisions was as follows:

1st Inactivated April 26, 1946 at Camp Kilmer, New Jersey.
Reactivated March 7, 1951 at Fort Hood, Texas.

2nd Has remained active since July 15, 1940.

3rd Inactivated November 9, 1945 in Germany.
Reactivated July 15, 1947 at Fort Knox, Kentucky as a training division and on March 15, 1955 as a combat division.

4th Inactivated March 4, 1946 in Germany.
Reactivated June 15, 1954 at Fort Hood, Texas.

5th Inactivated October 11, 1945 at Camp Kilmer, New Jersey.
Reactivated July 6, 1948 at Camp Chaffee, Arkansas.
Inactivated February 1, 1950 at Camp Chaffee.
Reactivated September 1, 1950 at Camp Chaffee.
Inactivated March 16, 1956 at Camp Chaffee.

6th Inactivated September 18, 1945 at Camp Shanks, New York.
Reactivated September 5, 1950 at Fort Leonard Wood, Missouri.
Inactivated March 16, 1956 at Fort Leonard Wood.

7th Inactivated October 9, 1945 at Camp Patrick Henry, Virginia.
Reactivated November 24, 1950 at Camp Roberts, California.
Inactivated November 15, 1953 at Camp Roberts.

8th Inactivated November 13, 1945 at Camp Patrick Henry, Virginia.

9th Inactivated October 13, 1945 at Camp Patrick Henry, Virginia.

10th Inactivated October 15, 1945 at Camp Patrick Henry, Virginia.

11th Inactivated September 30, 1945 in Austria.

12th Inactivated December 17, 1945 at Camp Kilmer, New Jersey.

13th Inactivated November 15, 1945 at Camp Cooke, California.

14th Inactivated September 23, 1945 at Camp Patrick Henry, Virginia.

16th Inactivated October 15, 1945 at Camp Kilmer, New Jersey.

20th Inactivated April 2, 1946 at Camp Hood, Texas.

ARMY RESERVE AND NATIONAL GUARD

Late in 1946 a number of tank and cavalry units were activated in the Organized Reserves, as this component of the Army was then called. These were one armored division (the 19th), four cavalry groups (the 301st through the 304th), two tank battalions (the 75th

The M37 (T76) Howitzer Motor Carriage was built on the chassis of the M24 Light tank.

(U.S. Ordnance Department)

An M8 Armored Car on Mindanao in the Philippines, 1945.

Amphibian and the 782nd), two cavalry reconnaissance battalions (the 314th and 315th), and one reconnaissance troop (the 83rd). Early in 1948 the name of the Organized Reserves was changed to the Organized Reserve Corps, and then in 1952 it was changed again to the Army Reserve.

The National Guard between World War II and the Korean War had two armored divisions (the 49th (Texas) and the 50th (New Jersey)), five armored groups, three cavalry groups, 31 tank battalions, and 15 cavalry reconnaissance squadrons. A tank battalion and a mechanized cavalry reconnaissance troop was organic to each of the 25 infantry divisions, and each infantry regiment had a tank company. Eight of the National Guard infantry divisions were called into Federal service during the Korean War.

By late 1955 the number of National Guard armored divisions had been increased to six by the conversion of four infantry divisions—the 27th, the 30th (that portion in Tennessee), the 40th, and the 48th. The North Carolina portion of the 30th became a full infantry division. At mid-1967 the National Guard, in addition to its six armored divisions, had two separate armored brigades, seven armored cavalry regiments, an armored cavalry squadron, and 16 separate tank battalions. Over and above this the 17 infantry divisions had 34 tank battalions and 17 cavalry squadrons.

THE COMBAT ARMS REGIMENTAL SYSTEM

In 1957, at the time of the first major reorganization of the U.S. Army divisions under the pentomic plan, there was a fundamental change in the organization of combat units. The arrival of nuclear weapons on the battlefield confirmed a trend that had started in World War II: the regiment, which had always been the basic fighting unit of the Army, was too large. Except in the case of the 2nd and 3rd Armored Divisions the armored regiments in 1943 had been broken up into separate battalions, many of which had lived their own individual unit lives unrelated to the regiments from which they stemmed. Many of the cavalry regiments, too, had lost their identities by being split up to form new units. Regimental history and tradition—so vital in any army—were scattered piecemeal across the mosaic of America's recent military exploits. The Combat Arms Regimental System (CARS) revived the old cavalry and armored regiments as parent bodies which would consolidate the relevant disparate units, including those which were inactive, and thus give a continuity to their regimental histories. Regimental headquarters were under control of the Department of the Army and each regiment could organize an average of some fifteen battalions or squadrons which would be activated as needed.

The parent regiments selected for use under CARS

An M8 Howitzer Motor Carriage passing a wrecked peep and a burnt-out Sherman. (U.S. Army 44–8780)

M26 Pershing being recovered by an M74 Armored Recovery Vehicle based on the M4A3 chassis. Pershings first saw combat with the 3rd and 9th Armored Divisions in Europe in 1945, and then in Korea. (U.S. Army)

Four U.S. tanks built in the 1950s. Left to right, M103 with 120-mm gun, M48 and M47 Patton with 90-mm gun, and M41 Light (Walker Bulldog) with 76-mm gun.

Newly modified at the Tokyo Ordnance Center in September 1950 this Sherman M4A3 was one of many which had its 75-mm M3 gun replaced by a 76-mm gun for use in Korea. The original turret was retained and the recoil guard of the 76 was modified to let it fit in.

(U.S. Army SC348719 Courtesy R. P. Hunnicutt)

were: the five armored cavalry regiments (the 2nd, 3rd, 6th, 11th, and 14th) whose structure was not changed under CARS, the twelve cavalry regiments (the 1st, 4th, 5th, 7th, 8th, 9th, 10th, 12th, 13th, 15th, 16th, and 17th), and seventeen armor regiments (the 32nd, 33rd, 34th, 35th, 37th, 40th, 63rd, 64th, 66th, 67th, 68th, 69th, 70th, 72nd, 73rd, 77th, and the 81st). Subsequently the Department of the Army decided that CARS cavalry regiments would contain reconnaissance type of units instead of tank battalions. This resulted in the redesignation of the 13th, 15th, and 16th Cavalry (tank battalion parent regiments) as the 13th, 15th, and 16th Armor. Those elements of the 5th, 7th, and 8th Cavalry which were assigned to the 1st Cavalry Division were not affected by this decision that cavalry should be reconnaissance type units and remained organized as infantry without any change in designation.

Most of the armor regiments had been armored regiments in World War II. Some originated at that time, others could trace their lineage back to the U.S. Tank Corps in World War I. All these armored regiments had been broken up in 1943, except the 66th and 67th in 2nd Armored Division which were not broken up until March 1946, and the 32nd and 33rd in 3rd Armored Division which were not broken up until July 1947. The other armor regiments (except the 15th and 16th) originated as separate non-divisional tank battalions in World War II.

The thirty-four parent regiments of armor and cavalry under CARS, with their date of original constitution, are:

Regiment	Date of Constitution (& Original Designation)
1st Cavalry (1st Regiment of Dragoons)	March 2, 1833 (as the United States Regiment of Dragoons)
2nd Armored Cavalry (Second Dragoons)	May 23, 1836 (as 2nd Regiment of Dragoons)
3rd Armored Cavalry (Brave Rifles)	May 19, 1846 (as the Regiment of Mounted Riflemen)
4th Cavalry	March 3, 1855 (as 1st Cavalry)
5th Cavalry (Black Knights)	March 3, 1855 (as 2nd Cavalry)
6th Armored Cavalry (The Fighting Sixth)	May 5, 1861 (as 3rd Cavalry)
7th Cavalry (Garry Owen)	July 28, 1866 (as 7th Cavalry)
8th Cavalry	July 28, 1866 (as 8th Cavalry)
9th Cavalry	July 28, 1866 (as 9th Cavalry)
10th Cavalry	July 28, 1866 (as 10th Cavalry)
11th Armored Cavalry (The Blackhorse Regiment)	February 2, 1901 (as 11th Cavalry)
12th Cavalry	February 2, 1901 (as 12th Cavalry)
13th Armor (13th Horse)	February 2, 1901 (as 13th Cavalry)
14th Armored Cavalry	February 2, 1901 (as 14th Cavalry)
15th Armor	February 2, 1901 (as 15th Cavalry)
16th Armor	July 1, 1916 (as 16th Cavalry)
17th Cavalry	July 1, 1916 (as 17th Cavalry)
32nd Armor	January 13, 1941 (as 2nd Armored Regiment)
33rd Armor	January 13, 1941 (as 3rd Armored Regiment)
34th Armor	August 28, 1941 (as 34th Armored Regiment)
35th Armor	January 13, 1941 (as 5th Armored Regiment)
37th Armor	January 13, 1941 (as 7th Armored Regiment)
40th Armor	January 13, 1941 (as 4th Armored Regiment)

63rd Armor	May 3, 1942 (as 745th Tank Battalion)
64th Armor	January 13, 1941 (as 78th Tank Battalion)
66th Armor (Iron Knights)	August 1918 (organized as HQ and HQ Companies of 1st and 2nd Provisional Brigades, Tank Corps, AEF)
67th Armor	September 1, 1929 (as 2nd Tank Regiment)
68th Armor	October 1, 1933 (as 68th Infantry (Light Tanks))
69th Armor	July 15, 1940 (as 69th Armored Regiment)
70th Armor	July 15, 1940 (as 70th Tank Battalion)
72nd Armor	January 14, 1943 (as 5th Armored Regiment)
73rd Armor	January 13, 1941 (as 76th Tank Battalion)
77th Armor	January 13, 1941 (as 73rd Tank Battalion (Medium))
81st Armor	August 28, 1941 (as 81st Armored Regiment)

Elements of these parent regiments have been organized in both the Regular Army and the Army Reserve, although not all those organized are active.

BIBLIOGRAPHY AND ACKNOWLEDGMENTS

DA Pam 672–1 Unit Citation and Campaign Credit Register WW II and Korea, July 6, 1961, with changes.

Forging the Thunderbolt, by Mildred Gillie, The Military Service Publishing Company, Harrisburg, 1947.

Army Lineage Series, Armor-Cavalry Part I, by Mary Lee Stubbs and Stanley Russell Connor, Office Chief of Military History, 1969.

The Development of American Armor 1917–1940, by Timothy K. Nenninger, Armor January–February March–April May–June September–October 1969.

It is trite phraseology to say that "without whose help this book could not have been written"; but in this case it is absolutely true. Without the research documents and correspondence of my friend Colonel Robert J. Icks, and the publications in the above bibliography, this account of the U.S. armored units and armored formations most certainly could not have been written. I am also greatly obliged, as ever, to Bob Icks for the photographs.

The 90-ton T28 Heavy tank resembled the German, Russian and British assault guns but was not available by the end of World War II.

(Photo Courtesy G. B. Jarrett)

M26 Pershing tank in Korea in the rôle of an artillery pill-box.

(U.S. Army Courtesy Col. G. B. Jarrett)

APPENDIX

As a result of the 1943 re-organization—which was not applied to the 2nd and 3rd Armored Division which remained as "heavy" divisions throughout the war, and was not applied to the 1st Armored Division until July 20, 1944, in Italy—the armored regiments in the armored divisions were broken up leaving three tank battalions in each division. The following examples show how these new tank battalions were formed and designated:

1st Armored Division: 1st (previously the 1st Armored Regiment less its 2nd Battalion which was disbanded)

4th (previously the 3rd Battalion and the Maintenance Company of the 13th Armored Regiment)

13th (previously HQ and HQ Company, Service Company, and Companies D, E, and F of the 13th Armored Regiment. The rest of the Regiment was disbanded, except for its Reconnaissance Company which was re-designated as Troop D, 81st Cavalry Reconnaissance Squadron, Mechanized, which was the division's cavalry reconnaissance squadron)

4th Armored Division: 8th (previously the 3rd Battalion of the 35th Armored Regiment)

35th (previously RHQ and HQ Company, and the 2nd Battalion of the 35th Armored Regiment. The 1st Battalion was re-designated as the 771st Tank Battalion, and the Reconnaissance Company as Troop D, 25th Cavalry Reconnaissance Squadron, Mechanized, which was the division's cavalry reconnaissance squadron. The Maintenance and Service Companies of the Regiment were disbanded)

37th (previously RHQ and HQ Company, the 1st Battalion, and Company D of the 37th Armored Regiment. The 2nd Battalion less Company D was absorbed in the 37th Tank Battalion. The 3rd Battalion was re-designated as the 706th Tank Battalion, and the Reconnaissance Company as Troop E, 25th Cavalry Reconnaissance Squadron, Mechanized. The Maintenance and Service Companies were disbanded)

5th Armored Division: 10th (previously the 3rd Battalion of the 34th Armored Regiment)

34th (previously RHQ and HQ Company, and the 2nd Battalion of the 34th Armored Regiment. The 1st Battalion was re-designated as the 772nd Tank Battalion, and the Reconnaissance Company as Troop D, 85th Cavalry Reconnaissance Squadron, Mechanized, which was the division's cavalry recon-

59

naissance squadron. The Maintenance and Service Companies of the Regiment were disbanded)

6th Armored Division: 15th (previously the 3rd Battalion of the 68th Armored Regiment)

81st (previously the 81st Armored Regiment less the 3rd Battalion, the Band, the Maintenance, Service, and Reconnaissance Companies. The 3rd Battalion was re-designated as the 707th Tank Battalion, and the Reconnaissance Company as Troop E, 85th Cavalry Reconnaissance Squadron, Mechanized. The Band and the Maintenance and Service Companies were disbanded)

68th (previously RHQ and HQ Company, and the 2nd Battalion of the 68th Armored Regiment. The 1st Battalion was re-designated as the 773rd Tank Battalion, and the Reconnaissance Company as Troop D, 86th Cavalry Reconnaissance Squadron, Mechanized, which was the division's cavalry reconnaissance squadron. The Band and the Maintenance and Service Companies were disbanded)

69th (previously RHQ and HQ Company, Regimental Medical Detachment, 1st Battalion HQ and HQ Company, and Companies A, B, C, and D. The 2nd Battalion less Company D was absorbed in the 69th Tank Battalion. The 3rd Battalion was re-designated as the 708th Tank Battalion, and the Reconnaissance Company as Troop E, 86th Cavalry Reconnaissance Squadron, Mechanized. The Maintenance and Service Companies were disbanded)

7th Armored Division: 17th (previously the 3rd battalion of the 31st Armored Regiment)

31st (previously RHQ and HQ Company, and the 2nd Battalion of the 31st Armored Regiment. The 1st Battalion was re-designated as the 774th Tank Battalion, and the Reconnaissance Company as Troop D. 87th Cavalry Reconnaissance Squadron, Mechanized, which was the division's cavalry reconnaissance squadron. The Band and the Maintenance and Service Companies were disbanded)

The M45 Medium tank, seen here crossing a river in Korea, was a modified Pershing armed with a 105-mm howitzer.

(U.S. Army Courtesy Col. G. B. Jarrett)

40th (previously RHQ and HQ Company, the 1st Battalion and Company D of the 40th Armored Regiment. The 2nd Battalion less Company D was absorbed in the 40th Tank Battalion. The 3rd Battalion was re-designated as the 709th Tank Battalion, and the Reconnaissance Company as Troop E, 87th Cavalry Reconnaissance Squadron, Mechanized. The Maintenance and Service Companies were disbanded)

9th Armored Division: 2nd (previously the 2nd Armored Regiment less the 1st and 3rd Battalions, Band, and Maintenance, Service and Reconnaissance Companies. The 1st Battalion was re-designated as the 776th Tank Battalion, the 3rd Battalion the 19th Tank Battalion, and the Reconnaissance Company as Troop D, 89th Cavalry Reconnaissance Squadron, Mechanized, which was the division's cavalry reconnaissance squadron. The Band and the Maintenance and Service Companies were disbanded)

14th (previously the 14th Armored Regiment less the 3rd Battalion, Band, and Maintenance, Service and Reconnaissance Companies. The 3rd Battalion was re-designated as the 711th Tank Battalion, and the Reconnaissance Company as Troop E, 89th Cavalry Reconnaissance Squadron, Mechanized. The Band and the Maintenance and Service Companies were disbanded)

19th (previously the 3rd Battalion of the 2nd Armored Regiment)

10th Armored Division: 3rd (previously the 3rd Armored Regiment less the 1st and 3rd Battalions, Band, and Maintenance, Service and Reconnaissance Companies. The 1st Battalion was re-designated as the 777th Tank Battalion, the 3rd Battalion as the 21st Tank Battalion, and the Reconnaissance Company as Troop D, 90th Cavalry Reconnaissance Squadron, which was the division's cavalry reconnaissance squadron. The Band and the Maintenance and Service Companies were disbanded)

11th (previously the 11th Armored Regiment less the 3rd Battalion, Band, and Maintenance, Service and Reconnaissance Companies. The 3rd Battalion was re-designated as the 712th Tank Battalion, and the Reconnaissance Company as Troop E, 90th Cavalry Reconnaissance Squadron, Mechanized. The Band and the Maintenance and Service Companies were disbanded)

21st (previously the 3rd Battalion of the 3rd Armored Regiment)

The modern U.S. Main Battle Tank M60A1E2, with the Shillelegh weapons system that can fire either conventional projectiles or missiles. The commander's cupola adds considerably to the otherwise low silhouette of the tank. The M60 was developed from the M48. (Col. R. J. Icks)

Index

32d Armor

33d Armor

34th Armor

35th Armor

37th Armor

40th Armor

63d Armor

64th Armor

66th Armor